Gold Bubble-eye

UK price
£4.95

Other titles of interest:

The Tropical Aquarium
Community Fishes
Coldwater Fishes
Marine Fishes
Maintaining a Healthy Aquarium
Garden Ponds
Aquarium Plants
Central American Cichlids
Fish Breeding
African and Asian Catfishes
Koi
Livebearing Fishes
Reptiles and Amphibians
Hamsters, Gerbils, Rats, Mice and Chinchillas
Rabbits and Guinea Pigs
Pet Birds

A FISHKEEPER'S GUIDE TO

FANCY GOLDFISHES

Red and White Ryukin

Chinese Lionheads

A FISHKEEPER'S GUIDE TO

FANCY GOLDFISHES

How to keep and enjoy a wide selection of these
popular and beautiful fishes in the home

Dr Chris Andrews

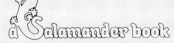
a Salamander book

Published by Salamander Books Limited
LONDON • NEW YORK

A Salamander Book

© 1987 Salamander Books Ltd.,
52 Bedford Row,
London WC1R 4LR,
United Kingdom.

ISBN 0 86101 278 X

Distributed in the UK by Hodder and Stoughton Services,
P.O. Box 6, Mill Road, Dunton Green, Sevenoaks, Kent TN13 2XX.

Ranchu Goldfishes

Credits

Editor: Geoff Rogers   Design: Kathy Gummer
Colour reproductions:
Melbourne Graphics Ltd.
Filmset: SX Composing Ltd.
Printed in Belgium by Henri Proost & Cie, Turnhout.

Author

Dr Chris Andrews is well known for his magazine articles and appearances on television in connection with the fishkeeping hobby. His interest in fish began with boyhood fishing trips to streams and ponds, and developed further as he kept a range of fish and other animals at home. After obtaining an Honours Degree in Zoology, he was awarded a Ph.D for his studies of fish diseases. He then spent eight years as a fisheries scientist for a Regional Water Authority and as consultant to a manufacturer of foods for the aquarium trade. In 1985, Dr Andrews took up the prestigious position of Assistant Curator (in charge of the Aquarium) at London Zoo, allowing his one-time hobby to become a challenging career.

Consultant

Pam Whittington was originally a Goldfish widow when her husband's hobby took him away to various meetings and shows. Her own involvement came later, but she has been a breeder and exhibitor in her own right for nearly thirty years, specializing in the London Shubunkin, with which she has had a long record of success on the show bench. Her other hobbies of gardening and photography are complementary to her fishkeeping activities.

Contents

Introduction

Millions of people around the world keep aquarium fish as a hobby. What is remarkable, is that many of these enthusiasts will have started by keeping a goldfish (*Carassius auratus*), a fish whose history can be traced back over 1500 years to Ancient China. The goldfish was once a rather drab-looking carp but, after patient breeding and cross-breeding over the centuries, it is now available in many different forms. These range from the familiar Common Goldfish to over 100 fancy varieties.

The first part of this book opens with a brief look at the history of the goldfish and its basic anatomy. From this point onwards, the text becomes entirely practical, with positive advice on how to keep goldfishes successfully in the home. The emphasis throughout is on making the right decisions from the start, i.e. choosing the appropriate size and shape of bowl or aquarium, ensuring that the water quality is correct, fitting the appropriate types of

filtration and aeration systems where necessary, providing suitable lighting if you aim to grow real plants, and decorating an aquarium safely and effectively.

Since fishkeeping involves recreating a living environment in the home, the time and care taken to start out correctly is more than repaid during the lifetime of the system. Having explained how to set up a bowl or aquarium, succeeding sections cover the vital activities of correct feeding and routine maintenance, plus a look at the exciting prospect of breeding goldfishes and rearing the fry to maturity.

Of course, disease and other problems can arise in even the best-regulated systems, and these aspects are also given full consideration. The final section of Part One explains how to take successful photographs of your prized fishes – a fitting preamble to the photographic survey of goldfish varieties in Part Two.

History and origins

The Goldfish (*Carassius auratus*) is without doubt the most popular pet fish in the world, and its association with the human race goes back 1600 years. It is the domesticated form of a small wild carp found in still and slow-flowing waters in Southern China, which resembles the European Crucian Carp (*Carassius carassius*).

During the Chin Dynasty (265-420 AD), Chinese fish breeders noticed that some of the rather drab green-brown local carp occasionally produced individual offspring with attractive red scales. Eventually, after patiently experimenting with breeding, they produced fish with more and more attractive coloration. By 1200-1300, silver, black, gold and even mottled fish were available, and these became quite popular as pets. By the late 1500s, variations in fin shape, such as fantails and veiltails, began to appear. These were followed by different patterns and body forms – and even new

History of the goldfish

China
Coloured wild fish 400AD.
Colour forms as pets by 1200.
Variations from 1600.

Japan
Introduced in 1500.
Breeding established by 1700.

Europe
Widespread during the 1700s.

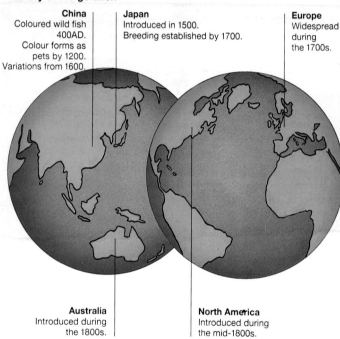

Australia
Introduced during the 1800s.

North America
Introduced during the mid-1800s.

China Coloured wild fish were observed around 400 AD. Various colour forms became available and were common as pets by 1200. Variations in body and fin shape appeared from about 1600.
Japan Goldfish were introduced from China around 1500. Breeding was established by about 1700 and was followed by the development of some fancy forms.
Far East Goldfish were widespread by 1700.

British Isles Goldfish were introduced around 1700.
Continental Europe Goldfish become widespread during the 1700s.
Russia Goldfish were introduced by the late 1700s.
North America Goldfish were probably introduced during the mid-1800s.
Australia and New Zealand Goldfish were introduced during the 1800s.

NATURAL SELECTION AND FISH BREEDING

Every species of animal continually produces 'mutations' among its offspring. These mutations should not be regarded as 'monsters', but rather as individuals often only showing slight physical or physiological differences from their parents and siblings.

Most frequently, these slightly different offspring are less well adapted for survival in their natural environment and they usually die before reaching maturity. Occasionally, however, the mutations may actually be better suited for survival, and therefore will be more likely to breed. They may produce offspring with similar advantageous characteristics.

This whole process is known as 'natural selection'. It results in gradual changes occurring in successive generations. As a result, the animals may become better adapted for life in their particular, and perhaps changing, environment.

In the case of the Goldfish, artificial selection by fish breeders, rather than natural selection by nature, has been the motive force for change. The Chinese fishkeepers of 1600 years ago noticed naturally occurring mutations among their native carp, and used these for selective breeding. Over many hundreds of years, selective breeding by fish breeders across the world has produced the many and varied types of fancy goldfish that we see today. All these varieties belong, of course, to one species (*Carassius auratus*) and they will all interbreed. In fact, the Goldfish will also interbreed with the closely related Crucian Carp.

It is interesting that when fancy goldfish are released into the wild, there is a gradual reversion to the green-brown wild form over a number of generations. The processes of natural selection and predation by other fish and birds quickly removes the more fancy and brightly coloured fish from the population. It is almost as if 1600 years of artificial selection can be undone in just a few years of natural selection.

eye shapes – by the 1600s. From this time onwards, further variations continued to appear in China and the interest in goldfish began to spread to other countries around the world.

Goldfish were taken to Japan, the home of the Koi carp (*Cyprinus carpio*), from China in around 1500, but it took another 200 years or so until goldfish breeding became established. Thereafter, Japanese fish breeders exerted their influence on this very variable fish, producing forms such as the lionhead and transparently scaled ('scaleless') variations such as the calico or shubunkin.

By the 1700s, goldfish had been introduced into many countries in the Far East. The opening up of trade and exploration routes around the world, together with the hardy nature of the goldfish and its ability to withstand long arduous journeys, no doubt aided the further spread of this fish around the world.

The goldfish first appeared in the United Kingdom in about 1700, or perhaps a little earlier. Around this time, the British began goldfish breeding, and some of the progeny were sent to continental Europe. Throughout the 1700s, goldfish were introduced from a variety of sources into Western Europe, and they reached Russia by the late 1700s. Interestingly, many of the more fancy types of goldfish did not appear in Europe until the 1900s.

The goldfish is thought to have been introduced into North

America during the 1800s, although some people claim that this occurred as much as 200 years earlier. However, by the late 1800s a goldfish farm was established in Maryland, USA, and recently goldfish have been recorded in the wild in every state except Alaska. The 1800s also saw the introduction of goldfishes into Australia and New Zealand, and the species is now widespread in natural waters in both countries.

Fancy goldfish can now be found in most, if not all, countries of the world. In many areas they have escaped or have been introduced into natural waters, where they have established feral populations.

Today, many millions of goldfish are bred every year on fish farms in North America, Europe and the Far East for distribution to fishkeepers around the world. This fish is known as 'chin-yu' in China, 'kingyo' in Japan, 'poisson rouge' in France and 'goldfisch' in Germany. Its hardy nature and bright coloration will continue to endear it to future generations of fishkeepers, who will enjoy the challenge of maintaining and developing the more fancy and bizarre varieties.

GOLDFISH FACTS

Family:
Cyprinidae (Carp family)
Scientific name:
Carassius auratus
Origins:
Southern China
Distribution:
Now worldwide, in aquariums, ornamental pools and natural waters.
Distinguishing features:
The Common Carp and the Koi Carp (*Cyprinus carpio*) both have barbels around the mouth. The Goldfish has none. The Crucian Carp (*Carassius carassius*) has no barbels, but generally has a deeper body and a longer dorsal fin than the Goldfish.
Size and growth:
A length of 20-25cm (8-10in) at 5-6 years of age is normal for goldfishes. Specimens up to 30cm (12in) long and weighing 4.5kg (10lb) have been noted.
Lifespan:
A lifespan of 10-20 years is not uncommon. Records exist of goldfish living for more than 40 years.

Pigmentation in goldfishes

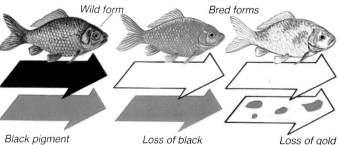

Wild form   Bred forms

Black pigment overlays gold

Loss of black reveals gold

Loss of gold reveals white

Above: Selective breeding has removed the pigment cells which give the wild goldfish (left) its drab colour. Further loss of pigment cells produce a white/ pink fish. When cultivated goldfish are released into natural waters, they revert to more sombre colours.

Below: Continued selective breeding has resulted in over a hundred varieties of goldfish, some showing evidence of the natural variation inherent in the wild goldfish population. This spectacular fish is a Pearlscale Veiltail Pompon Oranda.

Basic anatomy

The streamlined shape of the common goldfish is well designed for swimming through water. Since water is quite dense – about 800 times more dense than air – anything that helps the fish overcome this resistance is an advantage.

Selective breeding of fancy goldfish has resulted in fatter, less streamlined body shapes and has greatly modified the fins of some varieties. For both these reasons, many of the fancy varieties are relatively poor swimmers and less able to manoeuvre.

Here, we consider the main anatomical points of goldfish and review their bodily processes.

Skin and scales

The body of the goldfish is covered with scales, which help to protect it. These are easily lost with rough handling, but usually regenerate with time. A particular characteristic of the goldfish is the 27-31 scales along the lateral line running along the flanks of the body. (The number of scales along the lateral line is useful in the identification of some fish.) Goldfish scales are in fact transparent, and the coloration of the fish is provided by pigment cells in the skin underneath. Goldfish can be divided into three groups, according to how much reflective material is present in the skin beneath the scales. The groupings are as follows:

Metallic Fish with the full amount of reflective material in the skin. Such fish are often yellow, orange-red, silver, olive-green or even black, depending on the pigments in the skin.

Nacreous or calico Fish lacking some of the reflective material in the skin, giving the fish a pearly appearance. Nacreous fish may also have some metallic scales. As a result of the loss of some of the reflective material, a greater number of colours may be seen, including yellow, orange-red, silver, pink, black, blue and brown.

Matt Fish with no reflective material in the skin. This results in a very matt and sometimes scaleless appearance. As with nacreous fish, they are found in a wide range of colours, the most common being pink.

Always remember that the scales are covered with a layer of

Basic goldfish anatomy

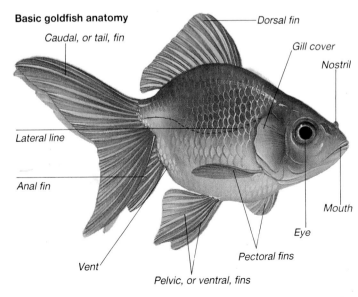

Caudal, or tail, fin

Dorsal fin

Gill cover

Nostril

Lateral line

Anal fin

Mouth

Vent

Eye

Pectoral fins

Pelvic, or ventral, fins

Above and left: *The paired pectoral and pelvic fins are used for making precise movements, the tail fin provides thrust, and the dorsal and anal fins give the fish stability.*

protective mucus, which is an excellent barrier against infection. When this mucus layer is damaged, by rough handling for example, the skin can become infected with a wide range of bacteria, fungi and parasites (see pages 58-64).

Fins and swimming

The common goldfish has three single fins – the dorsal fin, caudal or tail fin and anal fin – and two sets of paired fins – the pectoral fins and pelvic fins.

The dorsal and anal fins provide the fish with stability in the water and the caudal fin is used for swimming. Both the pectoral and pelvic fins are used for making quite precise manoeuvres.

Senses

Goldfish have the full compliment of senses, relying principally on sight, smell and hearing to locate food and detect the presence of obstacles and other fishes.

Eyesight

Goldfish have large eyes and quite good eyesight. Selective breeding has resulted in some striking modifications, including protruding or telescope eyes (see pages 83-88), and bizarre bladder-like swellings beneath the eyes, producing so-called 'bubble-eyes' (see pages 108-111). Such changes may impair the vision.

Hearing

Goldfish have quite good hearing, their 'ears' being internal structures in the head. Because of this, and because sound travels well through water, it is important not to knock on the glass of an aquarium. In common with other fish, goldfish are also able to detect very low frequency vibrations in the water by means of the lateral line system. This is made up of a series of small sense organs along each flank of the fish. These are sensitive to pressure waves in the water, helping the fish to detect other fish and obstacles.

Smell

There are two nostrils on each side of the head i.e. a total of four. These lead into a sensory pit which is responsible for the goldfish's sense of smell. In the Pompon variety of goldfish, skin outgrowths around the nostrils have been produced by selective breeding (see page 106).

Gills and respiration

Beneath the gill cover, or operculum, on each side of the head are four gill arches. Each gill arch supports a large number of finger-like gill filaments.Water is taken in through the mouth and forced over the gill filaments and out via the raised gill covers. As the water passes over the gill filaments, the fine blood vessels they contain absorb oxygen and release waste products such as carbon dioxide and ammonia. This process of gaseous exchange is similar to the process that occurs in the lungs of an air-breathing animal.

Since fish are 'cold-blooded' (more correctly known as poikilothermic or ectothermic), their body temperature fluctuates with that of the environment and they are more active – and thus require more oxygen – at higher temperatures. However, because warmer water frequently contains less oxygen than cool water, fish will show increased gill movements in warm, poorly aerated water.

Feeding and digestion

The downturned mouth of the goldfish indicates a tendency to feed at the bottom of the tank, although fishes will also feed at the water surface. Goldfish do not have teeth in their mouths, however. They feed by taking food in and then crushing it using the

Below: *A Calico Oranda, its mouth open to take in water that passes over the gills to provide oxygen and flush away waste products.*

Pharyngeal
teeth

Above: *Members of the carp family, including goldfishes, do not have rows of teeth in their mouths but 'pharyngeal teeth' in the throat.*

pharyngeal teeth at the back of the throat. The number and shape of pharyngeal teeth is useful in identifying certain members of the carp family. Unfortunately, they can only be examined in dead fish.

Digestive system

The goldfish, like many other members of the carp family, feeds on both animal and plant material. Its relatively long intestine helps the fish to digest plant material. By comparison, more carnivorous fish have much shorter intestines. There is no well-defined stomach in the goldfish, but more of a gradual change in appearance and function along the length of the alimentary tract.

Food taken into the mouth is crushed by the pharyngeal teeth, and passes into the first part of the alimentary tract. Here digestion begins, with the help of digestive juices and enzymes secreted by the fish. Once digestion is well under way, the products of this process are absorbed through the alimentary tract wall into the bloodstream and distributed around the body. The indigestible material passes along the alimentary tract and out into the water via the vent.

Since the body temperature of a goldfish is similar to that of its surroundings, the fish feeds more actively at higher water temperatures, while at lower temperatures it becomes dormant and its appetite wanes. Fishes can go for long periods without food and will come to no harm; in cold water they may cease to feed altogether.

Kidneys

In their freshwater environment, water is continually being drawn into the body tissues of goldfishes and, as a result, they rarely need to drink. However, the fish has to get rid of the excess water in its body and this process is carried out by the kidneys. These are situated beneath the backbone and run along the length of the body. They produce large amounts of dilute urine, which also contains salts and other waste products.

Swimbladder

The swimbladder is a large gas-filled bag divided into two roughly equal compartments. By adjusting the volume of air in the swimbladder, a goldfish can float at any depth, thus conserving the vital energy needed to maintain such a position in the water by active swimming.

Unfortunately, the selective breeding of fancy goldfish for particular body forms has altered the shape of the swimbladder so that it no longer consists of two roughly equal sections. This means that some fancy goldfish, especially the Pearlscale, are prone to swimbladder disorders that affect their ability to maintain their position in the water.

Reproductive organs

The reproductive organs – testes in the male, ovaries in the female – are situated just below the swimbladder. At breeding time these organs swell and give the fish, notably the female, a very rounded appearance. The male stimulates the female to shed her eggs into the water, where he fertilizes then with his milt, or sperm. Fertilization is thus external. (See pages 46-57.)

Bowl or aquarium?

You will have to decide early on whether you intend to keep your goldfish in a bowl or in a relatively spacious aquarium. In this section, we look briefly at the merits of each and review the basic principles of using them to maintain and display goldfish. In later sections, we concentrate in more detail on keeping goldfishes in an aquarium, with advice on maintaining water quality, providing lighting, choosing suitable plants and decoration, and carrying out regular maintenance.

A simple set-up
The simplest way to keep goldfish is in a bowl or in a small aquarium, both of which are now available in plastic. A wide-necked bowl or small aquarium is preferable than the old-fashioned glass globe, which has only a very narrow opening. Unless a globe is only half-filled with water, there will be a very small surface area of water exposed to the atmosphere for gaseous exchange.

Setting up a goldfish bowl or small plastic aquarium is very straightforward. Rinse out the bowl in clean water and then put in a layer of washed gravel and a small bunch of aquatic weed, a plastic plant or, perhaps, an ornament. The bowl is then ready for filling with tapwater. However, before adding the water, run it into a separate container and treat it with tapwater conditioner (to reduce the level of chlorine, other disinfectants and heavy metals,

such as copper) and bring it to room temperature by adding a little boiling water.

Float the goldfish, still in their plastic bag from the aquarium shop, in the bowl for 15-20 minutes, and then release them. This allows the temperatures inside and outside the bag to equalize so that the fish have a gentle introduction to their new home.

If your bowl does not have a suitable cover, you can easily make a cover to keep cats out by using a piece of fine mesh net held in place with an elastic band.

Maintaining a goldfish bowl
The bowl or small aquarium cannot really be looked upon as a balanced environment and is really suitable for keeping only two or three small goldfish. You can use an air pump to provide aeration, and filters are available for small aquariums and even fish bowls. Nonetheless, the small aquarium, and especially the goldfish bowl, will need regular and quite frequent cleaning, perhaps every two to four weeks. In fact, small bowls should be cleaned every week.

The best way to clean a bowl or small aquarium is first to transfer the fish and a little of the old water to a clean, detergent-free bucket. Then rinse the bowl, its gravel and all the ornaments in clean water, removing accumulated algae with a stiff brush. Wipe out the bowl or tank with a soft cloth, taking care

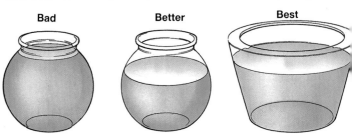

| Bad | Better | Best |

Above: *The surface area of water in a full narrow-necked design of goldfish bowl is unacceptably small. It is better to half fill a*

traditional bowl or opt for one of the modern wide-topped designs that provide a much larger air/water interface for gas exchange.

Above: A wide-top bowl with some gravel and a few strands of an oxygenating plant provides a fine home for two small goldfishes.

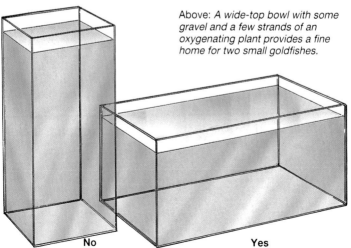

No

Yes

Above: These two aquariums hold the same volume of water but the horizontal design will support the greater number of fishes. This is because the safe stocking level for a particular tank is based on a simple correlation of water surface area to combined fish length.

to avoid scratching the sides if it is plastic. For this reason, avoid using razor blades and abrasive pads. You can try to remove stubborn algae and other deposits by using special tablet cleaners from aquarium shops, or by soaking affected items in a solution of sodium bicarbonate. Be sure to rinse these items thoroughly in clean water before replacing them in the bowl.

Refill the bowl with conditioned tapwater at room temperature. Then, after checking that the temperatures of the water in the bucket and the new water in the bowl are within a degree or two of each other, reintroduce the fish using a hand net or a small jug.

It is common practice to include a small bunch of aquatic oxygenating weed, such as *Egeria*, in the goldfish bowl. Generally, this does not survive very long and is sometimes eaten by the fish, but it may add useful oxygen to the water on bright days. However, the benefits of these plants are somewhat overstated and they can probably be dispensed with at no real risk to the fish.

Feeding goldfish is dealt with on pages 40-45, but suffice it to say here that bowls and small aquariums are very susceptible to the effects of overfeeding.

Using a larger aquarium

If you are interested to keep and breed a varied collection of goldfishes, consider setting up a larger aquarium. The most popular tank sizes are 60x30x30cm (24x12x12in) and 100x38x30cm (39x15x12in) in terms of length, depth and width. The first size will hold about 54 litres (12 Imp gallons/14.5 US gallons), and the second size approximately 104 litres (23 Imp gallons/27.5 US gallons).

So-called 'all-glass' aquariums are literally made of five sheets of glass, held together securely with silicone aquarium sealant and perhaps finished off with an attractive, but purely decorative, plastic frame. Modern tanks are

Above: *An undergravel filter, modest lighting, a combination of real and plastic plants, plus an ornament create a pleasing and viable goldfish aquarium.*

lightweight, relatively inexpensive and they rarely leak. Following a good rinse in clean water, they are ready for the fish.

Your local aquarium dealer will stock a range of different sizes and shapes of tank. The size of the tank, or more correctly the surface area of the water exposed to the atmosphere, is the factor which determines how many fish (and of what size) you can keep. As a guide, in a coldwater aquarium,

you should allow about 150cm^2 (24in^2) of water surface for each 2.5cm (1in) of fish body length, excluding the tail. As an example, a tank with a surface area of 60x30cm (24x12in) will support 30cm (12in) of combined fish body length. However, with modern methods of filtration and careful tank management, this figure can be increased substantially.

An aquarium may come complete with a cover and condensation tray. The cover is useful for keeping dust, household sprays and cats away from the fish and can be used for mounting lights. These lights are essential if you wish to grow real plants (see page 30). They are also very good for highlighting the attractive colours of the fish, especially if the tank is used to brighten up a dimly lit corner of the house. A clear plastic condensation tray will keep splashes and condensation away from the lights and electrical wiring around the aquarium.

If your aquarium does not come with a lid or hood, you can make a suitable cover from a sheet of glass or transparent plastic. You may need to cut away one or two corners to allow for airlines, filter wires, etc. going into the tank. Remember that the edges of a glass sheet must be smooth or covered with tape.

Water requirements and filtration

Most fishkeepers use tapwater to fill their tanks and bowls. Unfortunately, tapwater is intended for drinking rather than for fishkeeping and it contains a number of potential hazards for fish. Here, we consider how to ensure that the water we use in the aquarium is suitable for goldfishes and remains in good condition throughout the life of the system.

Conditioning tapwater

The hazards in 'raw' tapwater may include chlorine, chloramine and various dissolved metals, such as copper. None of these are toxic to humans at the levels normally found in tapwater, but they can be dangerous to fish. The simplest way to make tapwater safe for fishkeeping is to treat it with one of the easily available 'tapwater conditioners'. But be sure to use a 'complete' conditioner which not only eliminates chlorine, chloramine and toxic metals, but which also 'ages' new water in order to protect the fishes' delicate mucus membranes.

Today, a number of chemical filters, ion-exchange resins, de-ionising resins and even the old standby, activated carbon, can be used to alter or purify water. However, some of these can drastically change the chemical nature of the water, and can even make it too pure for the fish. Therefore, use such systems and chemicals with care.

For most purposes, suitably conditioned tapwater brought to the correct temperature is quite adequate for fancy goldfish.

Temperature

Do not forget that fresh tapwater will be a different temperature to the water in the goldfish bowl or aquarium. However, this can be adjusted quite easily by allowing the water to stand for a few hours at room temperature, or by adding a little boiling water from a kettle. Never add hot water directly to a tank containing fish. Always mix or condition water away from the fish; it is easier to adjust the results and

you will not harm the fish if you make a mistake. Avoid using hot water from the 'hot' tap as it may contain impurities from the pipework; draw water directly from the cold water mains instead.

Goldfish are very adaptable to water temperature, although be sure to avoid sudden changes at all costs. When changing part or all of the water in a bowl or aquarium, or when moving fish from tank to tank, always check that the temperatures are within a degree or two of each other. For the same reason, float new fish in their 'carry home' plastic bag in their new home for 15-20 minutes before releasing them. This will allow water temperatures to equalize.

A typical goldfish can survive temperatures ranging from near freezing to 30°C (86°F) or more, and thus is ideally suited for an unheated indoor aquarium. Of course, in an unheated room in temperate regions, the activity and appetite of the fishes will decrease during the autumn and winter period, but they will increase again during the following spring when temperatures rise.

The more 'fancy' varieties of goldfish require a more even temperature and they will suffer if it drops too low. In colder climates, especially if the tank is in an unheated room, it may be wise to install a heater-thermostat to prevent water temperatures falling below 12-15°C (54-59°F) during the winter period.

Acidity or alkalinity

The acidity or alkalinity of water is measured on a pH scale from 0-14. It is important to remember that each unit change in the pH scale is a logarithmic one, i.e. equivalent to a ten-fold change in the acidity or alkalinity. A pH of 7 is termed 'neutral'; a pH below 7 is 'acid'; a pH above 7 is 'alkaline'. Fish should never be exposed to sudden changes in pH of more than a fraction of a pH unit.

The pH value of tapwater can vary enormously, depending on where you live and the processes

Above: *Reliable kits for testing aquarium water chemistry, here nitrite level, are easy to use.*

carried out by your local water company. Goldfish are very adaptable and can live in a wide range of pH values, although it is best to avoid extremes. Try not to keep goldfish (especially fancy goldfish) in very acid or alkaline water, for example. A pH value within the range 6.5-8.5 is ideal.

You can measure the pH of your water quite simply using one of the widely available test kits. These usually involve adding a certain amount of a reagent to a measured sample of water from the tank and comparing the colour change to a printed chart. Paper strip indicators are also available to cover specific ranges of pH values. Using these is simply a matter of dipping the strip into the tank water and reading off the pH value by checking the colour of the strip against a reference chart printed on the pack.

Knowing your usual water conditions is very useful, since a sudden change in water chemistry may explain the onset of problems or unusual behaviour in your fish.

Water hardness
Water hardness is related to the amount of dissolved salts, chiefly calcium and magnesium, present in the water. Hard water contains large amounts of dissolved salts; soft water contains relatively few. Water hardness is measured by several different scales, including the widely used German scale of °dH. As a guide, water with a general hardness of less than 3° dH is 'soft', while water with a general hardness of 25° dH or above is 'very hard'.

Goldfish are very adaptable to various water hardness conditions, but try to avoid extreme or fluctuating conditions. You can measure water hardness with a test kit in a similar way to testing for pH value.

Ammonia, nitrite and nitrate
The natural processes of the nitrogen cycle convert nitrogen-containing wastes from the fish and uneaten food into ammonia (NH_3), then nitrites (NO_2^-) and eventually nitrates (NO_3^-). Ammonia and nitrites are more toxic to fish than nitrates, which may be used as a plant food. This whole process is made possible by the activities of millions of helpful bacteria and these form the 'operating system' of biological filtration in filters such as the undergravel and foam cartridge filters described on page 27.

In newly established tanks, however, only small numbers of these helpful bacteria are present. Until their numbers build up, which can take several weeks, the levels of ammonia and nitrite can become quite high, resulting in fish deaths – the well-known 'new tank syndrome'. Goldfish are quite hardy, but it is vital not to overlook the potentially harmful effects of high levels of ammonia and nitrite, especially in heavily stocked tanks with delicate 'fancy' forms or fry.

Once the tank and its filter are established, a number of factors can adversely effect the nitrogen cycle. These include oxygen shortage, some chemical treatments, a low pH value and low water temperatures. Any or all of these can result in temporarily raised levels of ammonia and nitrite, which in turn can be harmful to fish.

In order for the filter bacteria to function properly, they must be

The nitrogen cycle

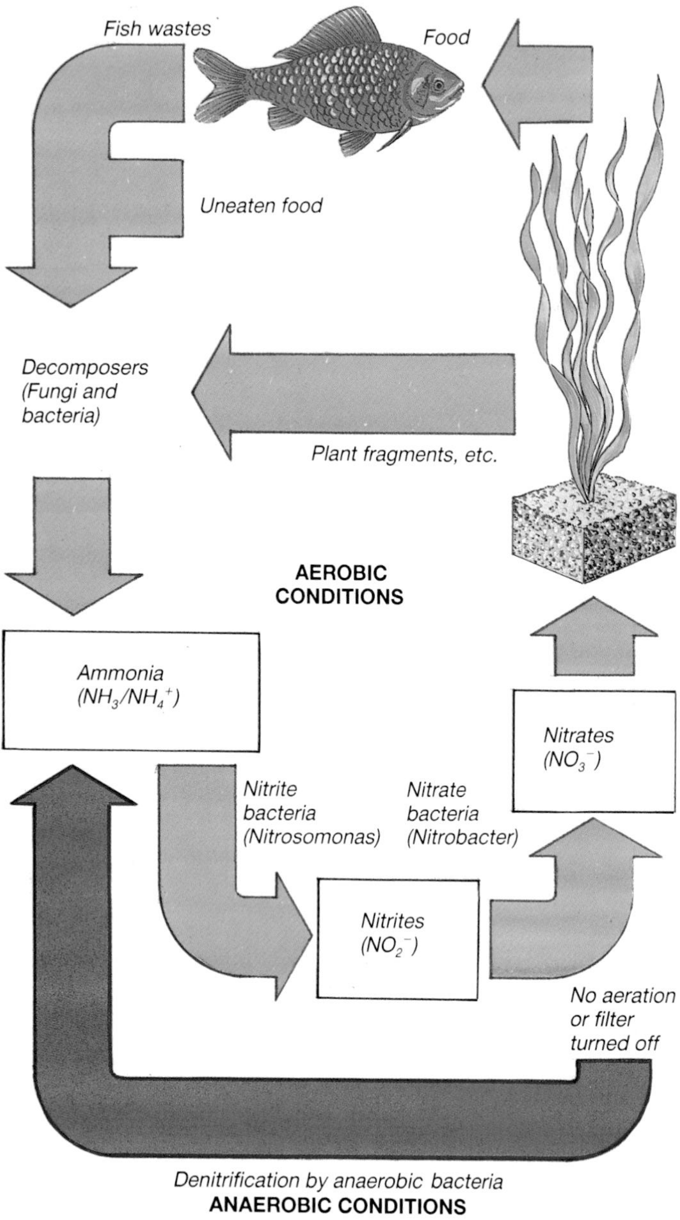

Fish wastes

Food

Uneaten food

Decomposers
(Fungi and
bacteria)

Plant fragments, etc.

**AEROBIC
CONDITIONS**

Ammonia
(NH_3/NH_4^+)

Nitrite
bacteria
(Nitrosomonas)

Nitrate
bacteria
(Nitrobacter)

Nitrates
(NO_3^-)

Nitrites
(NO_2^-)

No aeration
or filter
turned off

Denitrification by anaerobic bacteria
ANAEROBIC CONDITIONS

Above: The nitrogen cycle in the aquarium is responsible for converting potentially dangerous fish wastes and uneaten food into less toxic products, such as nitrate, which can be used as a fertilizer by the plants. The helpful bacteria responsible for this conversion process require a plentiful supply of oxygen to survive. Therefore, never turn off aquarium filters for long periods.

continuously provided with well-oxygenated water. This really means leaving the filters running most, if not all, of each day. However, turning them off occasionally for an hour or two will do no harm. This need for plenty of well-oxygenated water is the reason why regular filter maintenance is so important for efficient filtration.

Certain disease treatments, such as some antibiotics and methylene blue, can affect the filter bacteria. Do not use these treatments in heavily stocked tanks that rely on foam cartridge, undergravel or power filtration, unless you know that it is safe. Fortunately, most of the proprietary branded treatments now available have been developed for use in the aquarium without harming the filter bacteria.

In an established, well-maintained aquarium, there should be little or no ammonia or nitrite. Levels above 0.2mg/litre should be viewed with suspicion, and you should carry out a large-scale water change and try to establish the cause of the problem. Factors to consider include: poorly maintained filters, bad tank maintenance, overfeeding and overstocking. Ammonia is particularly toxic in water with a pH value of 8 or above, i.e. in alkaline conditions.

Filtration and aeration

Filters, air pumps and air stones are not usually used in the humble goldfish bowl. However, these devices can be very useful as they enable you to keep a higher stock level than would otherwise be possible, and they will maintain more stable tank conditions.

There is a vast array of filters, all with their own advantages and disadvantages. Three main systems are considered here, but whichever method you use, it is vital to leave them running for 20-24 hours each day and to clean and maintain them regularly.

Foam cartridge filters operate by drawing water through a foam cartridge which helps to remove particles from the water while at the same time breaking down fish waste and uneaten food biologically. These filters are easy to install and maintain, although they do require an air pump to drive them. Once a month or so, you should remove the cartridge from the filter and rinse it in lukewarm water before replacing it on the filter tube. This periodic cleaning prevents clogging and ensures efficient filtration in the long run. Unfortunately, foam cartridge filters are only really suitable for tanks up to 60-100cm (24-39in) in length.

Undergravel filters are very popular, mainly because they are cheap and easy to install, and unobtrusive in use. As the name suggests, they consist of a filter plate placed under the gravel plus various tubes necessary to set up a flow of water through the gravel and back into the main body of the tank. In the usual arrangement, water flows down through the gravel to the space beneath the filter plate, across the floor of the tank to a collecting tube or tubes that carry the water to the upper level of the tank. This flow can be set up either by using an air pump or by electrically powered water pumps (so-called 'power heads') fitted on top of the uplift tube or tubes.

The gravel bed should be made up of a 5-7.5cm (2-3in) layer of 2-3mm (approximately 0.1in) calcium-free gravel. This acts in a similar way to the foam cartridge by physically straining out particles of dirt as well as supporting colonies of bacteria that 'purify' the water. It is important to clean the gravel every month. You can do this either by 'vacuuming' the bed with a siphon tube or, better still, by using a 'gravel washer'.

Undergravel filters are a satisfactory means of filtering the goldfish aquarium, so long as the gravel bed is kept clean, but bear in mind that they may adversely affect plant growth. These filters can be used in almost any size of tank, although for best results the filter plate should cover most, if not all, of the tank bottom.

Power filters can be fitted inside or outside the tank. A high-powered water pump pushes the aquarium water through a canister containing one or more layers of filter media, which carry out both mechanical and biological filtration. No air pump is required, and power filters are usually very quiet. They are ideally suited to large, heavily stocked aquariums, where a high water turnover and good filtration is required, although the smaller types can be used in quite small tanks. The filter medium is often a foam insert, and this needs regular cleaning as described for foam filters. Other filter media, such as gravel, filter wool, pieces of ceramic piping and activated carbon can be used, although filters usually come with instructions on the best media to use for that model.

Power filters are now relatively easy to maintain, although some people may consider their appearance in or around the tank

Foam cartridge filter

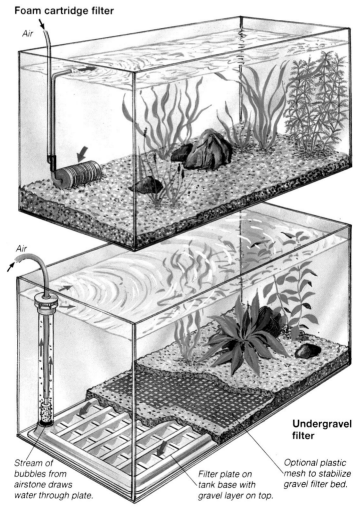

Air

Air

Undergravel filter

Stream of bubbles from airstone draws water through plate.

Filter plate on tank base with gravel layer on top.

Optional plastic mesh to stabilize gravel filter bed.

unattractive. However, they do provide a virtually silent and efficient method of filtration, especially for larger aquariums.

Aeration

Aeration is quite important in the goldfish aquarium since it helps to put much-needed oxygen into the water, as well as helping to drive off the carbon dioxide produced by the fish. When the water temperature increases and the fish become more active, they feed more, require more oxygen and produce more carbon dioxide. Since warm water contains less oxygen than cold water, aeration is especially important in heavily-stocked goldfish tanks during warm weather. Fish gasping at the water surface are a sure sign of oxygen shortage, signalling the need for at least temporary aeration. By their very action of setting up circulating water currents, foam cartridge and undergravel filters probably aerate the water sufficiently well on their own, but it is an easy matter to use the same air pump to power one or two airstones as well. The bubbles rising from an airstone add oxygen to the water (the mass of tiny air bubbles has a very large surface area), and the turbulence produced at the water surface helps gaseous exchange across the whole air/water interface. Many power filters come with aeration devices or spray bars, both of which are very useful for creating water turbulence.

Just as with aquarium filters, it is unwise to turn off aeration devices for long periods, especially during warm weather. Remember that although water turbulence is useful for aerating the water, many of the more fancy varieties of goldfish are not capable of dealing with very turbulent water conditions. For these fish, low stocking densities, and gentle aeration and filtration are recommended.

The filtration systems shown on these two pages – foam cartridge, undergravel and power filters – are all suitable for goldfishes. Be sure to maintain them regularly.

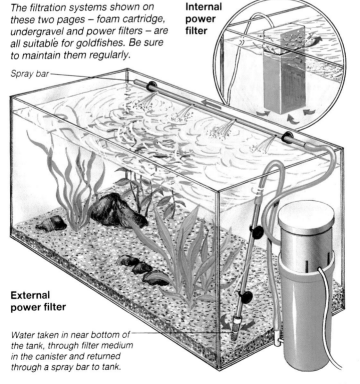

Internal power filter

Spray bar

External power filter

Water taken in near bottom of the tank, through filter medium in the canister and returned through a spray bar to tank.

Lighting, plants and decorations

A number of different forms of lighting are now available, including mercury vapour and metal halide lights, which produce a light closely resembling natural sunlight. They are excellent for encouraging plants to grow, but they do give off a lot of heat, which is often a disadvantage in the coldwater goldfish aquarium. For the same reason, ordinary household light bulbs are not ideal. A better choice would be to fit a fluorescent tube or tubes in the hood of the aquarium. These are supplied complete with all the fittings, starter units, etc. necessary for aquarium use. Once installed, these tubes are very cheap to run and do not give off much heat. They are available in a range of 'colours', including 'warm' tones, very white light, natural daylight and the pinkish glow

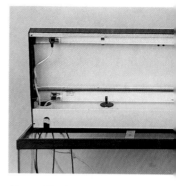

Above: *The 'pinkish' tube enhances fish colours; the white one provides overall illumination.*

Below: *Real plants, gravel and rocks create a natural look.*

Below right: *Coloured plastic plants and gravel look striking.*

produced by Grolux tubes. Grolux tubes are an excellent light source for encouraging plant growth and for bringing out the red coloration of fancy goldfish.

How much light?

If you wish to grow plants successfully, allow about 15-25 watts of fluorescent lighting per 30cm (12in) length of aquarium. Tanks less than 60cm (24in) in length will require less light than this, and tanks deeper than 45cm (18in) will need slightly more. Leave the lights on for about 10-14 hours a day, and renew the tubes about every nine months since the intensity of the light they produce gradually decreases with time. Where two tubes can be used, a combination of one 'cool white' and one Grolux tube produces a very attractive effect.

Very often, particularly where plastic plants are used instead of real ones, the lighting is only needed in order to view the fish. This is perfectly acceptable although, in the absence of real plants, algae may become more prevalent. To avoid encouraging algae, turn the lights on for only a few hours a day, perhaps in the evening. Anti-algae treatments are available from aquarium shops, but if a tank is badly infested, remove the worst of the algae using a scraper and siphon tube before adding the treatment. Tablets are also available to loosen encrusted algae on plastic plants and tank decorations. Algal control is also featured on pages 37, 64 and 65.

Plants

Generally speaking, except for the occasional bunch of oxygenating weed, such as *Egeria*, plants are not usually grown in the goldfish aquarium. This is because goldfish tend to be disruptive in a planted tank, and may even feed on some of the softer-leaved plants. Nonetheless, with proper tank lighting, the following plants can be used:

Ceratophyllum demersum – Hornwort
Egeria densa – Pondweed
Fontinalis antipyretica – Willow Moss
Ludwigia species – Ludwigia
Myriophyllum species – Milfoil
Sagittaria species – Arrowhead
Vallisneria species – Vallis

If you live in a warm part of the world, or if the tank is placed in a centrally heated room, you can also experiment with growing plants that would normally be used in the tropical aquarium.

To grow plants successfully, it is vital to provide adequate lighting. Sunlight, although excellent for encouraging aquarium plants to grow, cannot always be relied upon, and it will also encourage unsightly algae. Therefore, you will need to install some artificial lighting as already discussed.

Decorations

The choice of ornaments and materials for decorating the goldfish bowl or aquarium is enormous, although it is important to choose wisely. Do not use any rocks, gravel or other materials that will substantially alter the chemistry of the water. This usually means avoiding gravel or rocks containing limestone, since this will dissolve in the water and increase the hardness and raise the pH value, i.e. make it more alkaline. For similar reasons, avoid using cockleshell, coral, chalk and plaster of Paris. To detect limestone-containing rocks, test a small piece of rock with a few drops of dilute acid or vinegar. If tiny bubbles are produced, the rock contains limestone and you should not use it in the aquarium.

Above: *Real plants, light-coloured gravel and wood-grain decorations provide the perfect background for these splendid Ranchu goldfish.*

Slate, sandstone, granite and even coal are all ideal materials for decorating a tank, and your aquarium dealer should be able to supply natural, or even coloured, gravel that is limestone free.

You can also buy a range of other items for tank decoration, including artificial logs and rocks, plastic ornaments and plastic plants. All of these can be used, but avoid any rocks and ornaments with sharp or pointed edges which may damage the fish. Always wash any new items in plenty of lukewarm water and beware of any materials that release large amounts of dye into the water or that contain metals – unless you know they are safe to use with fish.

The tank should not be so cluttered that the fish cannot swim about freely. As a guide, it is often best if the rocks and decorations form a 'stage' against which you can view the fish, with plenty of open areas in the front and middle areas of the tank.

Aquarium backcloths and even dioramas (three-dimensional backgrounds) are now available for larger tanks. Since these need to be stuck onto the outside of the rear panel of glass, be sure to do this before the tank is filled and becomes immovable.

Other tank inmates

From time to time, other fish and animals are offered for sale in pet shops on the basis that they can be kept with goldfish. Some of the more hardy species of tropical fish, such as some livebearers (including Guppies and Platies), White Cloud Mountain Minnows (*Tanichthys albonubes*) and Ricefish (*Oryzias* sp.) will live in an unheated aquarium, as will fish native to Europe and North America. However, you should avoid mixing fish of very different

sizes and beware of keeping even small predatory fish with slow-moving fancy goldfish. Small Koi Carp can be kept in the goldfish aquarium, as can small freshwater lobsters and crayfish, but take care that these crustaceans do not attack the more fancy varieties of goldfish and small fry.

Snails are of no real benefit in the aquarium, although the Ramshorn Snail (*Planorbis*) is quite decorative and does little harm. These snails have flat, coiled shells measuring 0.3-2.5cm (0.1-1in) across. The Pond Snail (*Lymnaea*) can grow quite large and will eat aquarium plants, and is generally not recommended. As a result of their disruptive behaviour and 'nippy' habits, turtles and terrapins should also be avoided. Tadpoles will live in an unheated aquarium and will thrive alongside goldfish, so long as the fish are not too small or slow-moving. Tadpoles, of course, change into frogs and will eventually have to be provided with a terrarium or vivarium, and access to a dry area as soon as their front legs appear. For these reasons, bullfrog tadpoles are not recommended for the goldfish aquarium.

The goldfish, with all its varieties and colours, is a beautiful fish which deserves to be displayed in a tank of its own, free from the distractions of turtles, tadpoles – and even other species of fish.

Below: *Fish and aquarium decoration in perfect harmony – in this case an ideal setting for a Telescope-eyed Scaled Veiltail.*

Setting up and maintenance

This section summarises the basic steps in setting up a goldfish aquarium and reviews the ongoing responsibilities involved in routine maintenance.

Siting the aquarium

It is important to choose the site for your aquarium carefully, since it will be affected by a number of outside factors. Position it out of direct sunlight and draughts, and away from room heaters, all of which can cause undesirable fluctuations in water temperature. Furthermore, direct sunlight will encourage unsightly algae. Also be sure to keep pets and small children away from the fish.

Bear in mind that every 4.5 litres (1 Imp. gallon/1.2 US gallon) of water weighs about 4.5kg (10lb), and thus even a small aquarium will be quite heavy when filled with water. Consequently, be sure to provide a firm and even base. You can eliminate any irregularities in the surface of a table, shelf or stand by placing the aquarium on a thin layer of expanded polystyrene, such as ceiling tiles. Except for bowls and very small aquariums, it is important that you never try to move a tank which is full of water; always remove three-quarters of the water first. This will not only make lifting the aquarium easier, but will also prevent any damage to the tank seals.

When siting an aquarium, do not forget that you may need regular access to the top, the sides, and even behind the tank.

Establishing an aquarium

Once you have positioned the tank and equipped it with any necessary filters, lights and aeration equipment, you can fill it with conditioned tapwater at around room temperature and introduce a small number of hardy goldfish. These fish will help to get the tank properly established and you should not add any new ones for about a month or so. During this settling in period, carry out a weekly 25-50% water change, always refilling the tank with conditioned tapwater at the correct temperature to avoid thermal shock.

During this time, be sure to monitor the characteristic rise and fall in ammonia and nitrite levels – typical of the 'new tank syndrome' described on page 25 – using appropriate test kits. After four to six weeks, the filters and their helpful bacteria should be established, and then you can gradually increase the stocking density to about 2.5cm of fish length per 150cm^2 of water surface (1in per 24in^2) as outlined on page 23. Good filtration will enable even higher stocking densities of fish, but at first it is best to follow this simple stocking rule. Recurring outbreaks of disease, fish in poor condition, fluctuating water conditions, and the need for more than the usual amount of tank maintenance are all signs that the tank may be overstocked and/or underfiltered.

To avoid introducing unwanted disease organisms into an established set-up aquarium, it is probably a good idea to quarantine all new fishes for about three or four weeks. If you keep them in isolation in a small aquarium during this time, you can observe them for any sign of disease, and perhaps treat them with a broad-spectrum anti-parasite remedy to prevent problems later on.

Routine maintenance

One of the most important aspects of routine maintenance is to observe the fish each day so that you can react promptly to any early signs of problems or disease.

Keep the filters and air pumps running for most of each day, or the performance of the filters will be seriously reduced and the fish will be exposed to fluctuating water conditions. Since the goldfish aquarium is usually unheated, it is important to investigate the cause of fluctuating water temperatures.

Every two to four weeks, you should carry out a 25% water change, taking care to clean the

STEP-BY-STEP GUIDE TO SETTING UP A GOLDFISH AQUARIUM

Shopping list

Tank with cover
Filter and/or air pump with airline and airstone
Gravel
Rocks, decorations
Plastic plants
Real plants, where appropriate
Thermometer
Two hand nets
Tapwater conditioner
Siphon tube/gravel washer
Fish food
Test kits
Hood ⎫
Fluorescent light tubes ⎬ Optional unless real plants are to be grown
Starter unit ⎭
Fish in plastic bag from aquarium dealer

Essential steps

1 Rinse gravel in running water. Wipe out tank with a clean, damp cloth.
2 Position tank, checking that it is on an even surface. Put in undergravel filter plate (if you wish to use this form of filtration) then add gravel, decorations and plastic plants.
3 Connect filters/air pump. Add media to any power filters. Position filters/airstone in tank.
4 Record the pH and hardness of the tapwater. Fill the tank, taking care not to disturb the gravel and decorations. Bring the tapwater to room temperature with a little boiling water from a kettle; add tapwater conditioner. Check pH and hardness again.
5 Introduce real plants at this stage, ideally with the tank only three-quarters full to avoid overflow. Consider setting plants in small pots where undergravel filtration is being used.
6 Turn on filters/air pump and adjust flow if necessary.
7 Float fish in plastic bag for 15-20 minutes before releasing them – this will help to prevent any thermal shock.

Important notes

Only introduce two or three small fish at first; build up the stocking level over a few weeks.
Check local tapwater for pH value and hardness levels, which may be useful for future reference. Monitor the rise and fall of ammonia and nitrite levels in the new aquarium over the first four to six weeks.
Feed fish with special care during this early period.
Carry out a 50% water change every week for the first month or so; then a 25% change every two to four weeks.

gravel using a siphon tube or gravel washer. This will prevent a build-up of debris in the gravel. While the water level in the tank is temporarily low, this is a good opportunity to remove and clean any tank decorations, or to rearrange them. At the same time, you can overhaul and clean the power or foam filters as described on page 27, or as directed by the manufacturer.

Just as frequently, perhaps every few weeks, it is a good idea to check water conditions – such as pH, hardness and nitrate/nitrite levels – in the aquarium using reliable test kits. Of course, if problems do develop, you will need to monitor water conditions more closely than this. Always keep a record of the water conditions in the tank, and of the water used to fill it, as this information might be useful if problems do occur.

If you have fitted fluorescent tubes – perhaps in order to grow real plants in the aquarium – remember to renew them after nine months or thereabouts, as their output gradually decreases with time as explained on page 31.

Every year or so, you may wish to strip down the aquarium entirely, clean it out and refurbish it. When you do this, keep about half of the 'old' water and take

Right: *Cleaning the aquarium glass using a pair of magnetized abrasive pads will effectively remove the surface film of algae and dirt. Do this every 2-4 weeks.*

Below: *Algae filaments may build up in the tank for various reasons. Too much light is a common cause.*

CHECKLIST FOR A SUCCESFUL GOLDFISH AQUARIUM

● Initially, allow 150cm^2 (24in^2) of water surface for each 2.5cm (1in) of fish length, excluding the tail.

● Avoid sudden changes in temperature; do not keep fancy varieties below about 12°C (54°F).

● Avoid sudden changes in water chemistry, especially pH.

● Feed a balanced, varied diet; avoid overfeeding and tank pollution.

● Ensure adequate filtration and/or aeration at all times; service filters regularly.

● To grow plants, provide 15-25 watts of fluorescent strip lighting per 30cm (12in) of aquarium length; leave on for 10-14 hours per day.

● Change about 25% of the tank water volume every two to four weeks; top up with conditioned tapwater at the correct temperature.

● Remember that regular care and maintenance ensures a healthy, balanced aquarium.

care not to disturb the filter media too much with over-enthusiastic cleaning. This will help to reduce any water quality fluctuations when the tank has been refilled. Nonetheless, it is probably a good idea to carry out weekly 25-50% water changes for three or four weeks following a refit, and to keep a closer watch on the water chemistry for a while.

In temperate regions, and especially if the tank is in an unheated room, you will notice a seasonal decrease in the goldfishes' appetite and activity each autumn. This is normal, and simply reflects decreasing water temperatures. During the winter, the fish will require less food and, as a result, the tank will require less maintenance. Normal activity and appetite will return the following spring, when you should resume normal feeding and tank maintenance. Such seasonal changes will not occur in areas with less pronounced winters, in homes with central heating, or in tanks heated for the more fancy varieties of goldfish.

Right: *Use a gravel cleaning device at water changes; detritus is whisked away in the siphonic flow.*

Below right: *A simple goldfish bowl may need cleaning every week.*

MAINTAINING AN ESTABLISHED AQUARIUM

Maintenance task	Every day	Every 2-4 weeks	Occasionally
Check water temperature	●		
Turn lights on/off	●		
Feed fish	●		
Check fish behaviour	●		
Check filter and air pump	●		
Remove algae from rocks, decorations and tank glass		●	
Change 25% tank water while 'vacuuming' the gravel		●	
Clean or refurbish filter		●	
Measure pH, water hardness, and ammonia or nitrite levels		●	
Check electrical connections			●
Renew any fluorescent tubes			●
Refit tank following total strip down			●

Feeding

Aquarium fish depend upon their owner to provide them with a correct, balanced diet. This is vital, even for the hardy goldfish. A balanced diet provides the fish with energy and ensures adequate growth and the repair of bodily tissues. Correct feeding will also promote successful reproduction and will encourage maximum coloration and improve resistance to disease.

Goldfish are omnivores: that is, they eat food of both animal and plant origins. (Carnivores, such as the Piranha, feed upon other animals. Herbivores, such as certain cichlids, feed largely upon vegetable matter.)

Providing a balanced diet

A balanced diet should consist of proteins, fat or oils, carbohydrates, fibre, minerals, vitamins and trace elements, all present in the correct amounts. Too little or too much of certain nutrients can lead to problems.

Let us look at these basic 'ingredients' in more detail.

Proteins are complex nitrogen-containing compounds that are essential for the growth of young fish and for the repair of worn out tissues. These may be supplied from animal (e.g. fish meal) or plant (e.g. soya meal) sources, although it is easier for some fish to digest the former. Since fish cannot store protein in their bodies for use when supplies are short, it is important that the diet contains adequate amounts at all times. Proprietary fish foods vary in their protein content; it is typically 20-45%. Actively growing fish fry will require a diet containing a higher proportion of protein than slower growing or adult fish, so you should choose the food accordingly to allow for this.

The quality as well as the quantity of the protein is also important. Proteins are made up of a number of amino acids, some of which must be in the diet at all times. Even if a diet contains large amounts of protein but the protein is lacking in certain amino acids, nutritional disorders may develop. To help counteract this problem, the diet should include protein from a wide selection of sources. The good-quality flaked and other dried foods are suitable in this respect.

Fats or oils and carbohydrates are available from a wide variety of sources. They are important energy-producing foods. However, in contrast to protein, if a diet is too rich in these nutrients, the excess may be stored within the body of the fish. In extreme cases, this can have serious side-effects.

Fibre forms quite a large part of the diet for many omnivorous and herbivorous fish. In commercially prepared foods, it may also be used to add bulk to a diet that might otherwise be too concentrated and, perhaps, wasteful in use.

Vitamins, minerals and trace elements need only be present in relatively small amounts, although they are essential for a healthy balanced diet. Many fresh foods are a good source of these nutrients, as are high-quality prepared fish diets.

Proprietary foods

Today, a range of proprietary diets and other foods are available for all kinds of aquarium fish, including goldfish. These 'manufactured' foods can be broadly classified as dried, freeze-dried and frozen diets.

Dried foods such as flakes, pellets, sticks and tablets, are widely available and are convenient to use. If you buy good-quality brands, these can form the basis of the diet. The special goldfish foods available are ideal, but avoid using foods based largely upon biscuit meal, ants eggs and the like since they generally have a low nutritional value compared to other types.

Many types of dried foods,

especially flaked foods, feature special 'growth', 'colour' and 'vegetable' diets. Even though these may have been developed for tropical fish, their occasional use will add valuable variety to the goldfish diet.

Most dried foods have a limited shelf life and generally they should be used within a few months of purchase. Although they can still be used after this period, the vitamin levels decrease with time. Bulk buying of flaked foods, therefore, can sometimes be a false saving.

Freeze-dried and frozen fish diets are also available from aquarium shops. Although these have been developed primarily for tropical and marine fish, they are also useful for adding variety to the diet of goldfish and for

Above: *A Blue-scaled Telescope-eye eating a fragment of lettuce. Such items can add useful variety to a staple diet based on flakes and other prepared foods.*

conditioning brood fish for breeding. Convenient freeze-dried foods include *Tubifex* worms, mosquito larvae, bloodworms, *Daphnia* (water fleas) and brineshrimp (*Artemia salina*).

Live foods
A number of live foods can be used to add variety to the diet and to condition fish for breeding. However, their use brings with it a number of potential dangers. To begin with, feeding a restricted range of live foods, to the exclusion of all other kinds of foods, is unlikely to provide a balanced diet, and may even lead

to nutritional or other internal disorders for the fish. Do not, therefore, totally replace good-quality dried foods with live food. Furthermore, as many live foods originate from ponds, streams or rivers, they may bring with them aquarium pests, such as *Hydra* or snails, or even fish disease organisms. The risk of introducing disease organisms can be reduced by collecting live foods from fish-free water, but the possibility of introducing aquarium pests still remains. It may be safer to use live foods that do not live in water.

Here, we consider a range of live foods and discuss their merits and possible drawbacks in relation to goldfishes.

Earthworms are an excellent, and often overlooked live food for all

Below and below right: *These panels show a selection of suitable foods for goldfishes. Use them sparingly to provide a varied diet.*

kinds of fish, including goldfish. You can buy them from some pet shops and angling shops, but anyone who has access to a garden or patch of waste ground should be able to collect enough for their fish. In damp weather earthworms are easy to dig up, and worms will come to the surface of lawns after an evening shower of rain in the summer. In dry weather, you can keep your supply going by laying one or two damp sacks in a shady part of the garden and baiting the earthworms about once a week with some potato peelings or similar vegetable scraps. Earthworms can usually be found around manure heaps.

After collection, keep the earthworms for a few days in a sealed container. This should have small air holes for ventilation and a little damp grass or moss. During this time the worms will clean themselves of soil and wastes and will then be more palatable for the

DRIED FOODS

◄ **Pellets** Wide range that float or sink.

◄ **Foodsticks** Longer pellets that float.

Tablets Both ► sinking and stick-on types.

◄ **Flakes** Well-balanced staple diet.

Notes: High-quality dried foods can provide the basic diet.

FREEZE-DRIED AND FROZEN FOODS

◄ **Water fleas** Convenient freeze-dried form.

Bloodworms Larval midges; nutritious food.

Krill Marine shrimp. ► Best supplied in freeze-dried form.

Shrimps Smaller ► kinds can be fed in frozen form.

◄ **Tubifex cubes** Can be stuck on glass at any level.

◄ **Mosquito larvae** Excellent for conditioning fishes.

Notes: The benefits of live foods without the risk of disease.

fish. You can feed the worms whole or chopped, depending on their size and the size of the fish.

Sludge worms, such as *Tubifex* and other tubificid worms, are a live food familiar to most tropical fish hobbyists. These slim, centimetre-long, maroon worms are often used to tempt fish such as Discus to feed, and are given as a live food to adult breeding fish. *Tubifex* worms are not easy to culture successfully and so are most often obtained from an aquatic shop. Unfortunately, in nature these worms live in polluted stretches of rivers and streams, and it is from these unsavoury sources that most *Tubifex* are collected for aquarium use. Therefore, use *Tubifex* sparingly in the aquarium only as an occasional food rather than as a staple diet. Before use, rinse the worms gently in cold running tapwater for several hours and perhaps administer a preventative treatment with one of the liquid live food disinfectants available from aquatic shops. Once cleaned, you can keep *Tubifex* worms alive for some time in a shallow dish of cold water. Flush this through with fresh water every day or so.

Water fleas are tiny planktonic crustaceans, such as *Daphnia* and *Cyclops*. Like *Tubifex*, they are a popular live food among tropical aquarists. You can either buy them in small plastic bags from an aquatic shop or collect them with a fine hand net from a local pond in the summer months, when they 'bloom' rather like algae in a garden pond. You can feed them to larger fish fry or use them to condition adult fish for spawning.

However, like *Tubifex*, using water fleas as a live food may result in the introduction of unwanted pests or disease organisms. Unfortunately, *Daphnia* and related forms are less easily disinfected than *Tubifex*. Ideally,

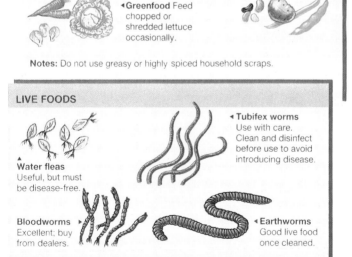

HOUSEHOLD SCRAPS

◀**Bread** A source of carbohydrates. Avoid white bread.

Peas and beans ▶ Nutritious foods. Use sparingly.

◀**Greenfood** Feed chopped or shredded lettuce occasionally.

Notes: Do not use greasy or highly spiced household scraps.

LIVE FOODS

▲ **Water fleas** Useful, but must be disease-free.

◀**Tubifex worms** Use with care. Clean and disinfect before use to avoid introducing disease.

Bloodworms ▶ Excellent; buy from dealers.

◀**Earthworms** Good live food once cleaned.

Notes: Ideal for variety but carry possible disease hazards.

therefore, obtain them from a safe fish-free pond or culture them yourself.

You can culture *Daphnia* in an old aquarium or plastic tub containing 20-30 litres (4.4-6.6 Imp gallons/5.3-7.9 US gallons) of tapwater that has been allowed to stand for 24-48 hours. Before adding the 'starter culture' of water fleas – obtainable from your local aquarium shop or pond – fertilize the water with a handful or so of manure (horse, cow or duck manure) tied loosely in a nylon bag. This will cause the water to go slightly cloudy after a week or so, signifying that the microorganisms on which the *Daphnia* feed have started to build up. Once this has happened, add the *Daphnia* starter culture and over the next few weeks their numbers will increase so that you can cull them several times a week using a fine-mesh net. Do not remove more than about 20% of the *Daphnia* at any one time, since this may deplete the culture beyond recovery.

The manure should provide sufficient nutrients to feed the water fleas for several weeks, after which time it should be replaced. Baker's yeast is another food for *Daphnia*. Add this in small amounts several times a week, taking great care to avoid overfeeding and fouling of the culture. The occasional lettuce leaf also seems to help.

Daphnia can be cultured outdoors in containers covered with glass or transparent plastic sheeting. They will thrive during the warmer months of the year, although they will go dormant during the winter. Alternatively, culture them indoors at around 20°C (68°F) with some overhead illumination and they will provide live food through most of the year.

Bloodworms are the aquatic larval stage of a two-winged fly. Difficult to culture, they are best obtained from aquatic shops and are particularly useful in the winter months, when other live foods may be scarce. Since they come from an aquatic environment, the above-mentioned health risks also apply to this live food.

Household food
With the development of commercial fish food, however, the need to offer fishes kitchen scraps and other household foods has all but disappeared. Nevertheless, some goldfish enthusiasts continue to feed their fish tinned peas, other vegetables, brown bread, etc., claiming that this is not only economical, but also of great benefit to the fish. Exercise care, however, to ensure that such foods are eaten and digested by the fish and are not allowed to pollute the aquarium.

Guidelines for feeding goldfish
During most of the year, you should feed goldfish two or three times a day with as much food as they will consume in a few minutes. You should soon be able to gauge the amount of food required. If you give too much food, the excess may accumulate in the tank, begin to decay and then either cause water quality problems or increase the need for tank maintenance. Each time you offer food, the fish should rise eagerly to the water surface. If not, this may indicate that they have been overfed, or that there is some other problem in the tank.

As we have seen on page 18, goldfish are 'cold-blooded' and take their body temperature from the surrounding water. This means that at higher temperatures they will be more active and require more food than at lower temperatures. The appetite of goldfish will decrease significantly as water temperatures fall below about 12°C (54°F), and very little food will be required below 8-10°C (46-50°F). This has obvious implications for the unheated goldfish tank in a house without central heating during the winter months, when food should be offered especially carefully.

As already mentioned, good-quality dried foods can form a staple diet for goldfish. However, two or three times a week, it is a good idea to offer a little freeze-dried, frozen or live food to add variety to the diet and help condition the fish, especially for breeding. The conditioning of adult fish for breeding and the foods needed for rearing the fry are discussed in more detail in the section starting on page 46.

Remember that many dried foods contain only about 10% water and are thus more concentrated than frozen or live foods, which may contain 70-80% water. This means that fish require surprisingly small amounts of dried food in order to remain healthy. It is also much easier to pollute the aquarium with dried foods than when using frozen or live foods.

Vacations

People who are not familiar with fishkeeping often imagine that aquarium fish are as much of a problem at holiday times as dogs and cats. Nothing could be further from the truth. As long as aquarium fish are cared for properly during the rest of the year, they will survive a one- or two-week vacation without needing any special attention or even feeding. Of course, you should leave the air pump and filter on for the duration of the holiday, and it is also a good idea to carry out a partial water change and to service the filter about a week before you go. There is no need to offer extra food during the week or so leading up to the holiday. Adult fish are quite well adapted to survive periods without any food and will not suffer unduly as a result of a temporary fast. Young fish fry, however, will need regular small meals every day. Vacation 'food blocks' are available for adult fish. These release small amounts as the block dissolves. Their use, which may ease the conscience of the absent fishkeeper, is largely unnecessary from the fishes' point of view.

If you cannot face the thought of leaving your fishes without food while you are away, leave precise instructions for your neighbours. Specify the amount of flaked food and the number of pellets or food tablets to be given, and how often. It may be a good idea to leave ready measured amounts of food for them to use. Be sure to impress upon them the dangers of overfeeding. Remember that the non-aquarist has a tendency to overfeed: emphasize the importance of the 'little but often' rule and point out that, generally speaking, hungry fish are healthy fish in the home aquarium.

While on holiday, you can leave any tank lights off during your absence unless there are real plants in the aquarium. If this is the case, consider fitting a time switch to turn the tank lights on for a few hours each day. This will not only prevent the plants from wilting but, if the lights come on in the evening, may also discourage burglars from intruding.

HOLIDAY CHECKLIST

One week before going away: Carry out a partial water change and filter maintenance. Feed normal amounts. Do not add any new fish for risk of introducing diseases which may cause problems while you are away.
The day before you leave: Check all the pumps, filters, etc. and leave them on while you are away. If necessary, measure out the required amounts of food and leave them in sealed containers for use by a neighbour.
While you are away: Your adult fish can survive quite well without food for at least two or three weeks, but you can let a neighbour feed them with pre-measured amounts if you prefer. Prevent overfeeding by hiding the remaining food!
On your return: Carry out a partial water change and filter maintenance. Resume feeding.

Breeding and rearing

Given the corrrect care and an adequate tank setup, it is quite feasible to breed goldfish in the home aquarium. Hobbyists should start with either the Common Goldfish or the Comet, leaving the breeding of more fancy strains until they have gained more experience. All goldfish belong to the same species, *Carassius auratus*, and will therefore interbreed. However, the uncontrolled crossing of different strains or varieties is not recommended unless it is part of a planned breeding programme.

Sexing goldfish

Goldfish often mature during their second year, but this will depend on diet, water temperature and other environmental influences. At the other end of the scale, you should not use fish that are older than four or five years for breeding purposes as they are probably past their prime.

In many temperate regions, the breeding season is in the summer. However, it is perfectly feasible to breed goldfish outside this period in semi-tropical areas or in an indoor aquarium.

During the breeding season, the body of the mature female will take on a full rounded appearance, especially when viewed from above. The mature male develops pale 'tubercles' – small bumps or pimples – on his head, gill covers and pectoral fins. This makes the male rough to the touch and he will use these tubercles to rub against the female during courtship.

The sex of goldfish can be confirmed by their behaviour at spawning time, when the male will actively chase the female for several days before spawning begins. Immature fish, or fish outside their breeding season, can be difficult to sex reliably.

Choosing the parent fish

It is vital that you choose the potential parent fish – or 'brood stock' – with care, since these fish

Below: Male goldfishes are usually slimmer than the females, with obvious white tubercles on the gill covers and head at spawning time.

will pass on their best – and worst – characteristics to their offspring. You will need one, or perhaps, two males to each female and you should, of course, avoid interbreeding different varieties. If necessary, you can prevent indiscriminate spawning by putting the males and females in separate tanks, or by keeping them on opposite sides of a tank divider.

Obviously, the brood stock must be healthy. They should show good finnage and coloration and should swim normally. Avoid fish with deformities, those which are noticeably slow growing, and any that were slow to change colour when juvenile. A willingness to feed is a good sign of a healthy fish in general terms.

Preparations for spawning
Correct nourishment is vital if your goldfish are to breed successfully. This means that in the few weeks

Below: *Two pairs of Ranchu spawning among Hornwort (Ceratophyllum). Such fine-leaved plants are ideal for breeding tanks.*

before spawning the fish need a balanced and varied diet that includes both good-quality prepared food and live food, such as earthworms and bloodworms. Naturally, you must resist the temptation to overfeed, which may result in an accumulation of uneaten food in the aquarium.

Aquarium breeding
Although goldfish will spawn of their own accord in outdoor pools, it is possible to control their breeding in an indoor tank. An aquarium measuring 60x30x38cm (24x12x15in) – these measurements refer to the length x depth x width – is the minimum size suitable for breeding goldfish. Long shallow tanks are more suitable than short deep tanks, since goldfish courtship can be quite a vigorous affair.
Ideally, position the aquarium where it receives some early morning sunshine, but away from full sunlight, room heaters and draughts. It is not necessary to cover the floor of the breeding tank with gravel, but you should put in

several bunches of fine-leaved plants, such as *Ceratophyllum*, *Myriophyllum* or *Fontinalis*. Goldfish will also spawn among 'spawning mops' made of bunches of nylon wool previously boiled to ensure that the dye colours are permanent. Install one or two sponge filters to provide filtration and aeration and it is a good idea to fit a secure lid to the tank.

One method of breeding goldfish is to place one or two mature males and a mature female in a breeding tank, but on opposite sides of a clear or perforated tank divider. The water temperature should be at least 15°C (59°F). In the evening, reduce the water depth to 10-12.5cm (4-5in) and remove the tank divider. Spawning should occur the next morning. If not, leave the fish together for a few days and if they still do not spawn, refill the tank and replace the partition. You can repeat this process after seven to ten days, when the fish may be more willing to spawn.

Reducing the tank water temperature by 2-3°C (4-5°F) can have a stimulating effect on the fish, especially if you add a few ice cubes to the breeding tank when you reduce the water level. However, you should avoid sudden temperature changes of more than the above amount.

After spawning, the eggs will look like pinhead blobs of jelly scattered among the weeds. Adult fish are notorious egg eaters and should be removed to another tank. A single female can produce several thousand eggs at one spawning. If she is allowed to recuperate away from the attentions of male fishes, and is given a good and varied diet, she will be able to spawn several times within a few months.

Eggs and young fry
Once the adult fish have been removed from the breeding tank, you should use a heater-thermostat to maintain a steady temperature of about 18-20°C (64-68°F). This will ensure the rapid, even development of eggs and fry. For the time being, keep the water depth at about 12.5cm (5in) and adjust the air supply to the sponge filters to give only very gentle aeration and filtration.

In these conditions, the eggs should hatch after four or five days. At lower temperatures, development will be slower and the eggs will take longer to hatch, thereby increasing the risk of egg

Below: *A tank set-up suitable for conditioning goldfishes for breeding. Place a mature male and female on either side of the tank divider. Remove the divider and lower the water level for spawning.*

fungus. This causes the eggs to become opaque and covered in a pale furry growth. If egg fungus is a problem with successive batches of goldfish eggs, you should add a proprietary remedy to the water of the breeding tank as soon as the adult fish have been removed.

Once the eggs hatch, the tiny fry will be very difficult to see. For approximately 48 hours after hatching, they hang motionless in the tank, not feeding, but surviving on the remains of the yolk from their eggs. Now is the time to ensure that you have a plentiful supply of the correct food to offer them, when they do start to feed.

About two days after hatching (or five or six days after spawning), you should start to offer the fry small but frequent meals of very fine food items. Infusorians and newly hatched brineshrimp are excellent first foods. Since it may take several days for the first cultures to mature, you should start one or two batches as soon as the adult fishes begin to show an interest in each other. In an emergency, you can feed newly hatched fry with chopped and

Top: *Goldfish eggs, which hatch in 4-5 days at 18-20°C (64-68°F).*

Above: *Newly hatched fry clinging to the side of the aquarium look like tiny slivers of glass.*

Below: *In good conditions, the fry grow rapidly and can reach a length of 2-3cm (0.8-1.2in) by the time they are six weeks old, as shown by these Calico fry. Feed them regularly with suitable foods.*

ground earthworms, or the yolk of a hard-boiled egg that has been squeezed through a fine muslin bag. (Use egg yolk sparingly; any excess will pollute the water very quickly.) You can also use a proprietary liquid fry food.

To ensure a rapid growth rate, illuminate the tank continuously for 24 hours a day and keep the water at a steady temperature (about 18-20°C (64-68°F), and offer several small feeds each day. Within just a few days, the fry should have grown sufficiently to take foods such as sieved *Daphnia* and proprietary liquid or dried fry foods. By giving the fry small but frequent meals you can ensure that their tiny stomachs are kept

These photographs show Calico Veiltails at different ages. At three months (right) the process of selecting the best fish should have begun. The five-month-old baby fish below has prize winning characteristics. The fishes at below right are eight months old.

FRY FOODS

Here, we look at how to culture live foods suitable for very young fry. Further guidance on feeding is given on pages 40-45.

Infusorians

Infusorians are tiny single-celled animals that occur in almost all water. They are an ideal first food for very tiny goldfish fry, and they can be cultured quite easily in containers such as large glass jars. To ensure a continuous supply, you will need to start a new culture every 3-4 days.

Three-quarters fill a jar with cooled boiled tapwater. Drop in three or four bruised lettuce leaves or a banana skin. You can even pour some boiling water over a little hay, in order to break up the cells, and add the hay to the jar. Place the jar, with the lid off, in a warm, moderately well-lit place. Over the next few days, the culture should go cloudy and begin to smell slightly. It will start to clear as the infusorians develop. Once the culture is clear and sweet-smelling, you can pour or siphon it into the fry tank, a little at a time.

Obviously, it is important to have the infusorians ready as the fry 'come on to feed', and to maintain a satisfactory supply until the fry accept other foods.

Brineshrimp

There can be few hobbyists breeding fish who have not heard of the brineshrimp (*Artemia salina*). This tiny saltwater crustacean is frequently used as a food for recently hatched fish fry. It is still the main standby for carp farmers when rearing very young fry. Brineshrimp eggs are available from most pet shops and aquarium stores. However, it is sometimes a false economy to buy them in bulk because, if stored in unsatisfactory conditions, the hatchability of the eggs will decrease markedly with

time. For best results, store the eggs in a cool dry place.

Culturing brineshrimp is relatively easy. You can buy a brineshrimp hatchery from a pet shop, but you can also achieve good results using several clean glass bottles.

Set up the 'bottle hatchery' in a warm room. The temperature should be at least 15°C (59°F), although the eggs will hatch more quickly – within 24-48 hours – at 20-25°C (68-77°F).

Pour about 400ml (approximately three-quarters of a pint) of cooled boiled water into a bottle. Add 8-12gm (about 2-3 level teaspoons) of cooking salt. (You may obtain better results using marine salts.) Aerate the salt water vigorously, then leave it to reach room temperature. Add about a quarter of a teaspoon (or less) of brineshrimp eggs. It is a good idea to put a cotton wool bung in the neck of the bottle. Remember that for the eggs to hatch successfully, they must be kept in warm, saline and well-aerated water.

One or two days after starting the first culture, set up a second bottle in the same way, followed by a third after another couple of days. The eggs will hatch after 24-48 hours in a warm room and, by starting several cultures in succession, you will ensure the availability of newly hatched brineshrimp for a week or so. By this time, the fry should accept finely powdered dried foods.

To separate the newly hatched brineshrimp from the egg shells and unhatched eggs, turn off the aeration for a few minutes. The living brineshrimp will collect in a layer about 2.5-5cm (1-2in) from the bottom of the bottle and can be siphoned out using a piece of airline. Top up the bottle with dechlorinated saline water, and turn the aeration back on. Each culture should last for 2-3 days.

full of food. You can check their progress using a hand lens. However, be sure to avoid overfeeding, and the consequent tank pollution, at all costs.

Since spawning, the fry tank has only contained about 12.5cm (5in) of water. After a week or two you can refill the tank to its maximum capacity, using conditioned tapwater brought to the correct temperature with a little boiling water from a kettle. Filling the fry tank before this can result in problems for the newly hatched fry, as they need easy access to the water surface to ensure the proper development of their swimbladders.

By three or four weeks of age, the fry should be feeding on good-quality powdered fry foods and crushed goldfish flakes or high-protein growth flakes.

Since goldfishes may produce large broods it is very important to provide adequate filtration and aeration in the tank and to carry out a weekly 25% partial water change. When there are small fry in the tank, a length of narrow-bore airline tubing makes a useful and safe siphon tube to drain water.

Rearing on and culling

Sometime during the first two to four weeks, you will have to reduce the numbers of fry. Discard any specimens that are very small or deformed, and pass on surplus fish to other hobbyists or to your local pet shop. Some fishkeepers find small goldfish an excellent live food for predatory fish, such as cichlids or marine Lionfish (*Pterois volitans*, for example).

By the time the fry are six weeks old they may have reached 2-3cm (0.8-1.2in) in length and you should establish a stocking density of 20-30 fish per 60cm (24in) tank. Do this by further culling so that you keep only the larger, more active and attractive fish. It is a mistake to try and rear too many fry in a small tank; it may seriously restrict their growth potential and may even jeopardize the whole brood if water problems develop or if there

is an outbreak of parasitic disease.

Clearly, selecting the best fish from a brood should be a continual process during the first few weeks. Your requirements and the tank space you have available will determine what proportion of the original brood you can keep and rear on. This may seem unkind, but it is similar to the natural selection process which happens in the wild. Culling, together with careful cross-breeding, is essential for the maintenance and development of the various strains of fancy goldfish. A humane way of culling small fishes is to drop them into a dish filled with ice cubes and place the dish in a freezer.

At about six months, the fish should measure 5-6cm (2.0-2.4in) long and some may begin to change from their bronze-brown colour to the more characteristic gold-yellow. Some goldfish may not change colour until 12 months of age. The timing of the colour change is determined in part by environmental conditions, such as temperature and diet, and partly by genetic factors inherited from the parent fish. Always choose brood stock from the fish that changed colour earlier than the rest.

Line breeding

As already mentioned, goldfish are available in over one hundred fascinating varieties. Since these varieties all belong to the same species they will, if given the chance, interbreed. However, interbreeding of different varieties is not recommended, since it usually results in a large proportion of poor-quality 'mongrel' stock. Ideally, you should begin by breeding common goldfish and then move on to the more selective and meticulous breeding of fancy varieties. Detailed information about the breeding of fancy goldfish is available in books devoted to the subject, and local Goldfish Societies are often very helpful. Here we provide a few general hints, but bear in mind that good-quality parent fish are essential if you want good-quality fry. Even then, you will need to cull a great many substandard offspring to end up with a small number of really splendid fancy goldfish from each brood.

Metallic-scaled varieties Select fry that change colour at an early age and reject any fish that have not changed by the time they are 12 months old. Deeper coloured fry are more likely to maintain their colour and produce offspring with a similar depth of coloration.

Nacreous or Calico varieties
Select fry that have the desired nacreous appearance, although it may take several months for the colours to develop. If a nacreous fish is not showing good colour by the time it is one year old, however, then it never will. Darker coloured fish seem more likely to maintain their colours with age. A streamlined body with well-developed and even fins is desirable in these fishes.

Fantails Both the anal fin and the caudal fin tail should be well divided into two matching halves. Choose fry that are deep bodied but not hump backed.

Veiltails The spawning of Veiltails often produces some Fantails. Select the fry with the longest fins, especially the anal fin. They should have a rotund body and an erect, strongly rayed dorsal fin. As with Fantails, the anal and tail fins should be well divided and evenly matched.

Moors Young Moors should resemble bronze Fantails. The black coloration and eye protrusion will develop with age. Discard any Moor that has not changed colour by the time the eye development is complete. In old age, Moors often develop a black velvety appearance, and some may even revert to orange metallic. One reason for this may be that the water temperature is too high, although it is important not to keep these fishes too cool.

Orandas and Lionheads The young fry must show the correct development of the fins and body. However, since the hood may take at least a year to develop, a roughened area on the head can be taken as a good sign. Avoid fish with uneven backs.

Celestials The eyes of Celestial varieties are normal in the young fish, but later they start to protrude sideways and then turn upwards. Select fry with good finnage and body shape and evenly developed eyes. The eyes take about six months to develop, although as with the development of features in many fancy goldfish, this period will often depend on the water temperature.

Bubble-eyes The eyes of this form are normal to begin with, but should have obvious 'bubbles' beneath them by the time the fish are about three months old. The back, which lacks a dorsal fin, should be evenly curved.

Pearlscales The characteristic pearly scale appearance of this fish develops at a very early age, making selection of fry quite easy.

Hand stripping
Healthy mature goldfish should, if left to their own devices, spawn quite readily on their own. However, goldfish, in common with salmon, trout and carp on fish farms, can also be spawned by hand. This may be particularly useful if you wish to carry out a very controlled breeding programme; if natural spawning only produces eggs of low fertility; or if egg eating by the parents or other fish is a problem. Some very fancy varieties seem to experience difficulty spawning on their own, and may need to be hand stripped as a matter of routine.

Before hand stripping, you must first condition the prospective parents in the normal way. It is vital to use only those fish that are already at the point of spawning naturally. Fish ready to spawn will

Hand stripping goldfish

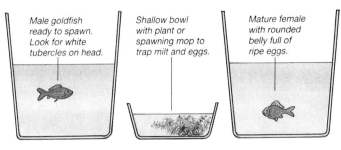

Male goldfish ready to spawn. Look for white tubercles on head.

Shallow bowl with plant or spawning mop to trap milt and eggs.

Mature female with rounded belly full of ripe eggs.

Above: *Before hand stripping, select a pair of fishes that are ready to spawn. Place the male and female in separate buckets*

and prepare a shallow bowl containing some aquatic plant or a synthetic spawning mop. Use tank water for buckets and bowl.

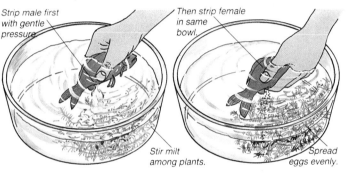

Strip male first with gentle pressure.

Then strip female in same bowl.

Stir milt among plants.

Spread eggs evenly.

Above: *Strip the male first. Hold the fish below water in the spawning bowl and expel a little milt by applying gentle pressure between the body and the vent.*

Above: *After gentle stirring to distribute the milt, repeat the process with the female straight away. Be sure to spread the eggs evenly around the spawning bowl.*

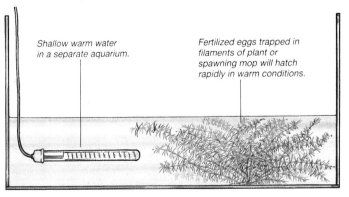

Shallow warm water in a separate aquarium.

Fertilized eggs trapped in filaments of plant or spawning mop will hatch rapidly in warm conditions.

Above: *After fifteen minutes, transfer the plant or spawning mop to an aquarium partly filled with water maintained at 18-20°C*

(64-68°F). The fertilized eggs clinging to the spawning medium should hatch in about four to five days at this temperature.

release eggs and milt easily. To try and force unready fish to spawn by hand may result in serious damage or even death.

Place the male and female fish in separate buckets, half-filled with water from the aquarium. You will also need to half-fill a small bowl with the same water and add to this some dense bunches of aquatic plant or spawning mops.

It is common practice to strip the male first. Catch the male in a soft net and with damp hands hold him under water in the bowl. Using the forefinger and thumb, apply gentle but firm pressure to the middle belly area and slowly move your fingers backwards towards the vent. A small amount of white milt should be expelled into the water. Return the male to his bucket and gently stir the water in the bowl to distribute the milt evenly. The milt will remain potent for only one or two minutes, so you need to work fairly fast.

Handling her in the same way, coax the eggs from the female fish and spread them around the bowl. Do not allow too many eggs to fall in one place and cluster together, as they will be difficult to separate and may develop fungus. You can then return the female to her bucket.

It may be possible to repeat the process two or three times with the same fish, although a new spawning bowl should be used for each release of milt and eggs. It is not necessary to strip the brood fish completely. Once you have collected sufficient milt and eggs, allow the fish to recuperate.

After ten to fifteen minutes, gently pour away the water from the spawning bowl, and transfer

Below: *Many amateur fishkeepers set up special fish houses to breed and rear fancy goldfishes. They produce high-quality fish for the show bench and aquarium dealers.*

the plants or spawning mops – complete with the now-fertilized eggs – to an aquarium containing shallow warm water. Healthy fertilized eggs will develop quickly, while infertile eggs will go white and will often contract fungus. It is not uncommon for some eggs to be infertile, although hand stripping should result in a quite a high percentage of fertile eggs.

Goldfish farming

Goldfish are now bred commercially on fish farms in many parts of the world, including the United States, Europe, the Middle East and the Far East. In most instances, the many millions of fish produced each year end up in pet or aquarium shops for sale to fish

Below: *A corner of a large outdoor pond used for breeding goldfishes. Goldfish farming is now carried out on a large scale in the USA, Europe, the Middle and Far East.*

hobbyists. In North America, however, there is a demand for goldfish to be used as bait by anglers.

On fish farms, goldfish are often allowed to spawn naturally in large outdoor ponds. The fry feed on plankton but, as a result of the very high stocking densities in the ponds, their diet has to be supplemented with dried foods. Under these circumstances, losses through cannibalism, predation and disease can be quite high. This method of fish production is not suitable for the breeding of high-quality fancy varieties, but it does result in economically priced 'bread and butter' fish. The breeding of fancy goldfish requires more care and attention, with much more rigorous selection of the better quality fish. As a result, such varieties are invariably more expensive and are often bred by dedicated amateur breeders who sell them on to the trade.

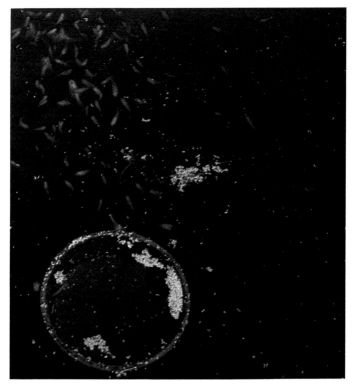

Pests, diseases and problems

Goldfish, like other aquarium fish, occasionally suffer from pests and other problems. While most of these can be prevented by proper aquarium maintenance, they can occur in even the best-kept goldfish bowls and tanks.

Infectious diseases
Fish are susceptible to a huge range of parasites and other infectious diseases, the effects of which are usually increased by overcrowding and inadequate aquarium care. Here, we review those particularly relevant to goldfishes.

Fungus (caused by *Saprolegnia* and *Achyla*) is a common disease among aquarium fishes, although it usually only affects fish that are already in poor condition for some other reason. The spores that give rise to the fungal infection are extremely common in water, but can only penetrate the skin of fishes that have been damaged by rough handling, fighting, spawning activity, or attack by other parasites.

If left untreated, the off-white or grey cottonwool-like fungal growth can spread rapidly across the body of the fish, eventually killing it. Consequently, prompt treatment with a proprietary fungus remedy is vital. Choose a medication which is added to the bowl or aquarium, as this is probably less upsetting for the fish. Very badly affected fish must be dipped into a strong solution of fungal treatment, but do this only in extreme cases.

White-spot disease (Ich) is caused by the protozoan parasite *Ichthyophthirius multifiliis*. It is transferred directly from fish to fish, and can therefore build up quickly within the confines of a well-stocked aquarium. It is relatively easy to diagnose, as it appears as small white pimples – about the size of sugar grains – on the skin, fins and gills. Heavily infested fishes will scrape themselves against rocks in an irritated fashion, and may suffer

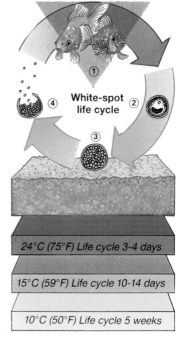

White-spot life cycle

24°C (75°F) Life cycle 3-4 days

15°C (59°F) Life cycle 10-14 days

10°C (50°F) Life cycle 5 weeks

Above: *1. Parasites beneath skin (resistant to treatment). 2. Mature parasites break out and form cyst. 3. Parasites divide. 4. Free-swimming stages re-infect fishes.*

from secondary fungal or bacterial infections in their weakened state.

White-spot is usually introduced into the aquarium with new fishes, or with live foods or plants. Thus, a two- to three-week period of quarantine, together with treatment with a proprietary white-spot remedy, is a good preventative measure for all new fishes. As an additional precaution, you should only use safe live foods (see pages 41-44) and give all plants a good rinse in clean water before putting them in the aquarium.

Fortunately, there are a number of safe, effective white-spot treatments widely available from aquarium shops. Using one of these as soon as the first spots are seen usually brings the condition under control.

Sliminess of the skin is related to the presence of large numbers of

Above: *Signs of white-spot can be seen developing on this Moor. Treat this parasitic infection promptly with a proprietary remedy available from your dealer.*

parasites on the skin, and sometimes on the gills. These include protozoans such as *Chilodonella*, *Costia (Ichthyobodo)*, *Cyclochaeta (Trichodina)* and even white-spot (*Ichthyophthirius*), as well as flukes such as *Gyrodactylus* and *Dactylogyrus*. When present in large numbers, these parasites irritate the skin of the fish, causing excess mucus production – hence the name of the disease. Affected fishes can be seen rubbing against the gravel or decorations in an agitated fashion. Other symptoms may include reddened areas on the body, closed fins and increased gill movements.

Sliminess of the skin can cause death, or can weaken the fish so that it succumbs to other disease organisms. Treat promptly with a white-spot remedy or a broad spectrum anti-parasite medication.

Finrot is usually the result of a localized bacterial infection which can be brought on by a number of factors, including fin-nipping, overcrowding, unhygienic tank conditions and low water temperatures.

The fins appear split and ragged, and may be streaked with blood or show reddening at the fin bases. As with all diseases, prompt treatment is very important, and there are a number of proprietary brands of general fish tonics which are effective against finrot.

Both finrot and fungus can be good indications that conditions are less than satisfactory in the aquarium, and both infections require immediate attention from the aquarist.

'Hole-in-the-body' disease is often caused by a systematic bacterial infection. This spreads through the body of the fish and manifests itself as ulcers, reddened areas on the skin, raised boils, and reddening at the fin bases and the vent. Other symptoms are listless behaviour,

lethargy and loss of appetite. This disease may be brought on by incorrect care, although new and recently spawned fish are also particularly susceptible.

Fish showing signs of this disease should be isolated from other fish, and should be treated by feeding with an antibiotic medicated flaked food or by adding antibiotics to the water. (You may need a veterinary

prescription for antibiotics.) Large aquarium fish can be injected with an antibiotic preparation, although this must be carried out with the cooperation of a veterinarian. Once the symptoms subside and the fish begins to behave normally, it can be returned to the aquarium.

Mouth fungus, which is caused by the bacterium *Flexibacter*, often occurs in newly acquired fishes or

Above left: *Symptoms of finrot, fungus and mouth fungus – often seen on fish in poor condition.*

Above: *Protruding scales and a swollen belly – signs of 'dropsy', commonly a bacterial infection.*

Left: *Clear signs of ulcer disease, a bacterial infection. It requires prompt antibiotic treatment.*

those kept in unhygienic conditions. The disease organism can destroy the mouth region of badly affected fish, and hence prompt treatment is vital.

Mouth fungus may respond to treatment with proprietary remedies from an aquarium shop, and more difficult cases can usually be cured by adding antibiotics to the water.

Fish pox is a problem which frequently affects Koi, but seems to trouble goldfish and other species less frequently. The symptoms are a white, pinkish, or even grey waxy growth on the skin and fins. The growth tends to appear, develop and then disappear, perhaps to recur at a later date.

The growth is produced by a viral infection in the cells of the fish's body. The infection may lay dormant for many months but, unfortunately, we do not fully understand what triggers off viral multiplication and the characteristic 'pox' symptoms.

However, fish pox does not appear to be very infectious and does not seem to pass easily between fish. The disease rarely, if ever, causes serious problems. It is unsightly rather than dangerous and fishkeepers must learn to put up with it for the time being, since there is no reliable treatment.

Leeches are very obvious, but relatively uncommon parasites. They can, however, be a serious problem. Not only do they feed on the blood and tissue fluids of the fish, but they also transmit certain microbial diseases between fish and allow secondary invasion with fungus or bacteria at their point of attachment. (Not all 'leeches' are parasitic, and there are many free-living, leech-like scavengers which may be found in aquariums or ponds.)

If you see parasitic leeches attached to your fish, be sure to take prompt action before the leeches build up in number.

Because of their powerful suckers, leeches cannot usually be removed with forceps without first getting them to loosen their grip using a strong salt solution. You can transfer the heavily infested fish to a treatment bath containing a three percent salt solution (30gm of cooking salt per litre of water/ approximately 24 level teaspoons per gallon). Leave the fish in the salt solution for a maximum of 10 minutes. Those leeches which do not fall off the fish can be removed with forceps. Kill the leeches by immersing them in boiling water. Alternatively, some anti-parasite medications may prove effective against leeches.

Fish lice (*Argulus* sp.) are another type of large fish parasite that no fishkeeper can fail to diagnose properly. About 0.5cm (0.2in) across, these flattened, disc-shaped crustacean parasites can be found on the skin and fins of affected goldfish. Fish lice can move about on the body of the fish, and can also live away from the host for short periods.

With their piercing and sucking mouthparts, *Argulus* fish lice irritate their host so intensely that heavily infested individuals will often leap out of the water in an attempt to get rid of the lice. Like leeches, these lice also transmit various microbial diseases, and the wounds left by their mouthparts may become invaded with fungus. Fortunately, effective treatment is quite easy using broad spectrum anti-parasite remedies.

Anchor worm (*Lernaea*) is a relative of *Argulus*, and may be found on goldfish from time to time, especially on newly acquired fish. Looking like a 1-2cm (0.4-0.8in) long piece of straw protruding from the flanks, fin bases or head region of the fish, this parasite is usually easy to spot, although low-level infestations may be overlooked.

Heavy infestations will seriously debilitate the host fish, and a reddened boil-like lesion can

Above: *Parasitic leeches weaken the host fish by feeding on its blood and body tissues. The skin damage they cause may become infected with fungi and bacteria.*

develop at the point of attachment. Treatment involves removing the parasites with a pair of tweezers, while holding the fish in a damp cloth. You should also disinfect the aquarium with a suitable proprietary remedy.

Non-infectious conditions
Here, we discuss swimbladder disorders of fancy goldfish, 'pop-eye' and external or internal growths, before considering pests and water quality problems.

Swimbladder disorders can usually be recognized by the inability of the affected fish to maintain its position in the aquarium; it either floats to the surface or sinks to the bottom. In less severe cases the fish may swim with a pronounced 'list'. Sudden changes in temperature are often cited as a cause of swimbladder disorders. Fancy goldfish seem particularly prone to the problem, and this may be related to the deformed shape of the swimbladder in the more fancy varieties, as mentioned on page 19. The condition does not appear to be infectious.

There is no reliable cure for this problem, although keeping the fish in shallow water maintained a few degrees warmer than the aquarium sometimes offers some respite. Naturally, fish showing symptoms of a swimbladder disorder should

HINTS FOR TREATING GOLDFISHES

1 It is usually safer and easier to treat diseases by adding a reliable proprietary remedy to the water in the bowl or aquarium.
2 Calculate the volume of the tank or bowl carefully. Tank length x width x water depth (measured in cm) and divided by 1000 equals the volume in litres. Divide this figure by 4.5 for Imperial gallons or by 3.8 for US gallons. Deduct 10% from the volume to allow for any gravel, tank decorations, etc.
3 Turn off activated carbon filters during treatment.
4 Do not overcrowd fish during treatment and ensure adequate aeration.
5 Always try out a remedy on one or two specimens before treating a whole batch of delicate or expensive fish.
6 Excessive amounts of organic matter will reduce the effectiveness of most remedies.
7 Never mix remedies unless you know it is safe. Carrying out a 50-75% water change or using an activated carbon filter for 12-24 hours should remove most of the active ingredients after each treatment is finished.
8 Remember that correct care and prompt treatment are vital for healthy fish.

not be used for breeding and fish that are no longer able to feed should be painlessly destroyed.

'Pop-eye' is an apt name for a condition in which one or both of the eyes protrude from the head of the fish in a very unnatural fashion. (Note that certain fancy varieties of goldfish are purposely bred with protruding eyes.)

This problem is rarely infectious, and often seems to cause the fish very little discomfort. Since there is no reliable treatment, and so long as the fish continues to feed and behave normally, there is no need to take any action.

Growths or tumours appear as obvious lumps on the outside of the body or as hard swellings among the internal organs. They are rarely infectious. External tumours can be removed surgically by a veterinarian, but treatment of internal growths is virtually impossible.

However, there is at least one parasite infection that produces a condition known as 'kidney bloat', where the kidneys swell and the belly of the fish becomes grossly distended. This disease, on the other hand, is infectious and is almost impossible to treat.

Below: *Swimming at an unnatural angle or an inability to maintain a level position in the water may be a sign of a swimbladder problem.*

Because kidney bloat is easily confused with a tumour, all fish showing tumour-like growths should be isolated from the rest of the stock. So long as the fish continues to feed and otherwise behaves normally, keep it in isolation and observe it for signs of improvement. If at any time the fish appears to be suffering unduly, it is best to destroy it painlessly.

Below: *Skin tumours are relatively uncommon and are not usually infectious. Surgical removal by a veterinarian is possible.*

Bottom, opposite bottom: *Internal swellings can be tumours or, as shown here, caused by the 'kidney bloat' parasite,* Mitraspora.

Pests and problems

A number of pests may occur in the goldfish bowl or aquarium from time to time.

Algal problems, including excessive growth of green 'hair' algae and 'green water', are often caused by the scarcity of living plants in the aquarium, too much light and overfeeding. Conversely, an unsightly growth of brown algae may develop under poor lighting conditions.

While a small amount of algae in an aquarium does no harm, and may actually enhance its appearance, too much will be a problem. Remove excessive algal growths with a scraper and siphon tube, and rinse the tank

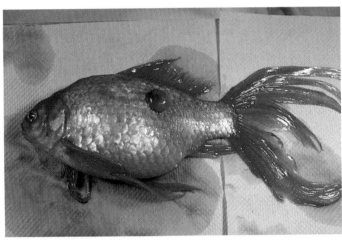

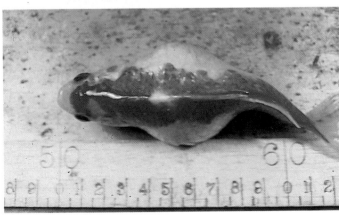

Above: *Although this Ramshorn Snail* (Planorbis) *will pose no threat to adult goldfishes, try to avoid harbouring snails in the aquarium.*

Above: Hydra, *here just visible attached to a leaf, is harmless to adult fish but the stinging cells on its tentacles can kill fry.*

decorations in tapwater. In a set up and carefully maintained aquarium, it may be worthwhile adding an anti-algal treatment to the water, as well as reducing the amount of food offered to the fishes. In an aquarium with no real plants, or only a few, you should reduce the amount of light. Use the tank lights solely for viewing the fish in the evening, and avoid long periods of exposure to natural sunlight, as sunlight greatly encourages algal growth.

With sensible feeding, regular tank maintenance and careful control of tank illumination, it should be possible to control algae without the continual use of chemical remedies. However, you should avoid stripping down the tank too frequently as this will disturb the important balance between the fish, algae and light.

The same guidelines also apply to the goldfish bowl, but the same sort of balance can never develop in such a small and highly artificial environment. Algal problems in bowls are best avoided by regular and thorough cleaning, and siting the bowl away from direct sunlight.

Hydra are small freshwater anemone-like creatures which are often introduced into aquariums with food. When disturbed, the body contracts from its extended length of up to 2.5cm (1in), thus disguising its characteristic tentacled appearance. Using the tiny stinging cells in their tentacles, *Hydra* prey on live food, small fish and fry in the aquarium.

Since *Hydra* are most likely to be a problem in the fry tank, the best method of control is good tank hygiene and careful selection of live food. Badly infested fry tanks should be stripped down and thoroughly cleaned by washing all the equipment in a dilute solution of bleach, followed by a good rinse in tapwater. *Hydra* are unlikely to pose a threat to larger goldfish.

Snails are by no means essential inhabitants of a goldfish aquarium and, since some species may become pests, avoid introducing them into a tank. Rinse all new plants in running water before putting them in the tank.

Chemical snail eradicators do exist, but use them carefully, especially in a badly infested tank, where the sudden death of a large number of snails may lead to water pollution. Even when present in large numbers, snails are unsightly rather than dangerous to fish. If all else fails, it may be necessary to strip down the tank completely, wash all the rocks, gravel and decorations in dilute bleach, and then rinse them thoroughly in tapwater.

Flatworms and bristleworms are often introduced into the aquarium with live food. These free-living worm-like creatures up to about 3cm (1.2in) in length thrive in unhygienic, dirty conditions; uneaten food and accumulated organic matter encourage these pests. Rather like snails, they are unsightly rather than harmful, although they may attack fish eggs and fry. To control these pests, avoid overfeeding, carry out more frequent partial water changes, remove any accumulated food and debris, and ensure that you maintain and clean the filters regularly as recommended.

Water quality problems
As we have seen, goldfish can tolerate a wide range of water conditions. However, in spite of their hardy nature, a number of problems can result from incorrect water conditions. For a more detailed review of water requirements and filtration, see pages 24-29. Here, we recap on a few common water quality problems that may arise.

Tapwater Tapwater is fine for the aquarium, but condition it first using a good-quality 'complete' conditioner, which will remove chlorine, chloramine, metals, etc. Use a conditioner at every water change and avoid sudden changes in water temperature.

Ammonia and nitrite problems
The nitrogen cycle converts nitrogen-containing waste products, uneaten food and plant fragments to ammonia, then nitrite and eventually to nitrate. This process is made possible by the activities of helpful bacteria, and forms the basis of biological filtration. In newly established tanks, however, only small numbers of these bacteria are present. Until their numbers build up, which can take several weeks, the ammonia and nitrite can reach quite high levels, resulting in the well-known 'new tank syndrome' losses.

Once the tank and its filter are established, a number of factors can have an adverse effect on the nitrogen cycle. These include shortage of oxygen, chemical treatments and low temperatures.

Above: *Always treat 'raw' tapwater with a good-quality conditioner to reduce levels of chlorine and other 'disinfectants' in the water.*

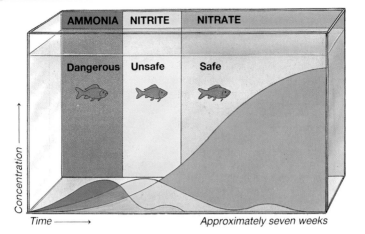

Above: *In new tanks, toxic levels of ammonia and nitrite are produced in overlapping 'peaks'. Once the filters are established and nitrifying bacteria start to break down these substances, less toxic nitrate is produced. Control nitrate with partial water changes, at weekly intervals for the first few weeks.*

In order for the filter bacteria to function properly, they must be provided with well-oxygenated water at all times. Therefore, biological filtration systems should be left running most of the time, although turning them off for an hour or so occasionally will not cause much harm. Since these filters usually become clogged with accumulated debris, cleaning them regularly is important for long-term efficient filtration. The gravel bed of an undergravel filter should be regularly 'vacuumed' with a siphon tube, or cleaned using a gravel washer. And remember to rinse filter sponges in lukewarm water every two to four weeks.

Certain disease treatments, such as some antibiotics and methylene blue, will harm the helpful bacteria in the filter. Do not use these treatments in a heavily stocked tank with biological filtration, unless you know it is safe to do so. Fortunately, many of the proprietary treatments have been developed for use in the tank without harming the filter flora.

Filter bacteria prefer warm, neutral-to-alkaline water; they do not function very well in water cooler than 10-15°C (50-59°F) and with a pH value of less than 7.0. Keep a close check on ammonia and nitrite levels in heavily stocked goldfish tanks. Carry out regular partial water changes and consider using zeolite – a chemical filter medium available as off-white chippings – to absorb any excess ammonia present in the water.

Cloudy water When a goldfish aquarium is first established, it is not uncommon for the water to turn rather cloudy. However, it should clear after a week or so as the tank and its filters become properly established. Persistent problems with cloudy water can be related to a number of factors, including:

1 Overfeeding. The water may smell rather unpleasant and ammonia and nitrite readings may be high.
2 Inadequate or poorly maintained filters.
3 Over-vigorous aeration and the disturbance of excessive amounts of tank debris.
4 A 'green water' algal bloom. (See pages 37, 64 and 65 for details of controlling algae.)
5 Frequent tank stripdowns, which prevent the system from becoming completely established.

Showing

Sooner or later, many enthusiastic goldfish keepers want to find out more about their fish, exchange ideas with other hobbyists – and perhaps even enter one or more fish in a local fish show. Aquarium dealers and the monthly aquatic magazines available from newsagents should provide information on nearby fish clubs, as well as details of the more specialist organizations.

Competitive showing
Competitive showing is often one of the most important activities of a local fish club and quite prestigious prizes can be won at regional, national and international levels. At local club level, the show is often divided into a number of broad – and usually taxonomic – groupings or 'classes', such as characins, cichlids, anabantoids, etc. There are usually a number of specific fancy goldfish classes, as well as classes for other coldwater fishes. This type of local 'mixed' show is a good place for the fishkeeper to obtain experience in the art of showing fish to their best advantage, before going on to exhibit at larger or more specialist goldfish shows.

The organization of each show may vary, and so, if you are new to showing, it is best to contact the show organizers a few weeks in advance. This will allow you plenty of time to check on the classes available at the show; the show standards for each class of fish; entry fees; precise show times; the regulations governing tanks for exhibiting the fish, etc. Fish at shows are often exhibited in a special small all-glass tank provided by the owner of the fish and there may be strict rules about tank size and the tank decorations (if any) that may be used.

You can transport the fish to and from the show in rigid plastic buckets with a tight fitting lid or in double-layered plastic bags inside a sturdy box. If the fish are packed carefully and not exposed to fluctuating temperatures, they will survive a journey of several hours

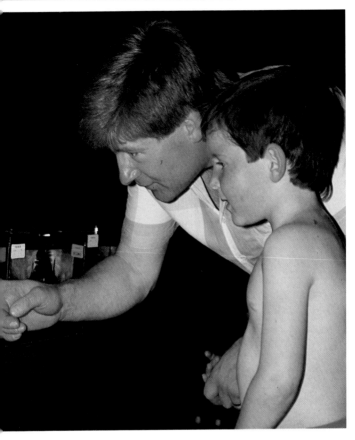

Left: *Fish are judged on the basis of specific characteristics. Sound knowledge of these 'show standards' is required for success.*

Above: *Fish clubs and fish shows, cater for people of all ages and interests, and provide a marvellous insight into this absorbing hobby.*

without any problems. A local aquarium dealer or fish club should be able to offer advice on fish transportation. Small battery-operated air pumps can be very useful for aeration purposes.

Be sure to check the fish that you intend to show against the standards of the class for which they are to be entered. Attempting to enter a fish in the wrong show class will simply result in disqualification. The body proportions and form, colour and finnage, as well as the overall size of the fish, are all important factors to consider. Naturally, these are likely to vary – at least slightly – for

the different classes of fancy goldfish.

Not only must an exhibition fish conform to the standards for that class accepted by the club, but it must also 'exhibit' well! This means that it must be used to being handled, moved from tank to tank, confined in a relatively small show tank, and so on. In fact, championship fish quickly adapt to these conditions and may travel hundreds (if not thousands) of miles from show to show during a season.

Although it is frowned upon by some fish hobbyists, showing is the life-blood of many fish clubs.

Fish photography

In many ways, goldfish are an ideal subject for photography. They are colourful and available in a range of body shapes, with various types of finnage. They are also relatively large and quite slow moving, enabling the would-be fish photographer to take a little longer composing each picture.

Basic equipment
The basic equipment you will need is a 35mm camera, a flashgun and, preferably, a relatively fast film (i.e. 200-400 ASA/24-27 DIN). The quality of fast films has improved and they no longer produce the grainy photographs of early films. They allow a greater depth of focus, especially if you are working with close-up lenses. Fast films thus offer advantages over slower films (100 ASA or less) without any major drawbacks.

To appreciate goldfish to their fullest extent, you should use colour film, but the choice between prints or slides is yours. Bear in mind that it is easier to convert slides to prints than vice versa and, if you are thinking of submitting your work for publication, remember that magazine and book publishers usually prefer slides.

While reasonable results can be obtained using a small 35mm compact camera, you will get better photographs using a single lens reflex (SLR) camera. Not only do these cameras allow through-the-lens focusing, but they also enable you to get closer to the subject, even without special lenses. As you become more involved in fish photography, you will find the SLR camera more flexible than a compact camera, permitting the use of a whole range of lenses and filters.

The choice of SLR camera will be governed largely by cost, although the more expensive models are not necessarily better suited to fish photography. A local camera shop or photographic club can be a source of helpful advice as well as reasonably priced secondhand cameras. Do choose a camera that is compatible with a wide range of different lenses, and that can be combined with a compatible (or 'dedicated') flashgun. Fully automatic cameras may appear attractive to the beginner, but there is a danger that without a manual override facility, you may suffer from a lack of flexibility as you become more experienced.

Above-tank lights on their own will seldom be sufficient to allow an adequately fast exposure to 'freeze' the movements of even quite slow-moving fish. The use of special photographic spotlights is not considered here, since not only do they give off large amounts of heat that will warm the water and can cause discomfort to the fish, but they are also unlikely to be available to most amateur fish photographers. A flashgun is, therefore, the best option and it will instantly 'freeze' on film the movements of even very active fish. However, using a flashgun brings with it at least one significant problem: reflection.

Most flash units are either housed within the camera body, or are mounted on top of the camera. If the camera is used at right angles to the glass panel of an aquarium, the reflection that rebounds from the flash will all but obscure the subject of the photograph. Therefore, holding the camera, and hence its flash unit, at an angle of about 45% to the glass, will prevent the flash rebounding directly into the camera. Alternatively, in some models you can remove the flashgun from the camera and, using an extension lead, position the flashgun either above the tank or at a suitable angle to the glass. This will enable you to keep the camera at right angles to the tank. However, good results can still be achieved with the flash unit left on the camera simply by avoiding reflection through careful positioning.

Although it is not an essential piece of equipment, a tripod is very useful. After a short time, even the smallest camera can feel quite heavy, especially if you are waiting for a fish to adopt a particular pose. A tripod which permits good all-round movement of the camera will provide you with a degree of manual freedom, and will prevent your photographs turning out blurred through tired and shaking arms.

Taking the photograph

You may wish to photograph your fish in their normal aquarium. This can be a time-consuming process, but the results are often more natural. Furthermore, if you want to photograph breeding and feeding then the fish will almost certainly need to be in their own aquarium.

However, it is quite simple to set up a photographic tank and use it for staged portrait shots. A 45x25x25cm (18x10x10in) tank is adequate and can be used to

Below: *Restraining the fish inside a smaller tank within the main aquarium or in a separate tank will facilitate taking photographs. If the inner tank is not open to the air, react promptly to signs of distress caused by oxygen shortage.*

Tank set-ups for fish photography

Ideally, set up a separate tank for 'portrait' photography. Keep the front glass clean and use a power filter to clarify the water.

'Mini tank' open only on one side to confine subject against the front glass.

Add decorations and/or backdrop as required.

Raise the mini tank off the bottom to avoid including the floor of the larger aquarium in the photograph.

Prepare a 'simulated' gravel bottom in the mini tank by setting a layer of gravel in silicone aquarium sealant.

photograph quite large fish. It should be made of glass, silicone sealed, and should have no visible scratches on the front pane. Fill it either with water from the stock tank, or with conditioned tapwater at the correct temperature. A glass cover will help to prevent splashing and unless, the fish is to be kept in the tank for some time, aeration and filtration will be unnecessary. To remove any suspended matter in the water use a high-turnover power filter for an hour or two. You can decorate the tank with well-washed gravel, rocks, plants and so on. An aquarium backcloth, or even a diorama (three-dimensional background), fixed to the outside of the rear panel can be used for extra effect.

During a photographic session, it is vital not to subject the fishes to extreme temperature changes and to handle them very carefully. Use a soft net to catch the fish and ensure that they are not unduly stressed.

Photographing a small fish can be a problem, unless it is gently confined to the front of the tank. To do this, construct a glass 'mini tank' measuring, say, 20x10x10cm (8x4x4in). You can decorate the bottom side of the tank with gravel set into a layer of aquarium sealer. Lay this tank on its side, close to the front glass of the tank, with the chosen fish inside. Make sure that all of the air is excluded. Rest the confining tank on a flat stone or brick to prevent the bottom edge of the main tank appearing in the photograph.

In this way, the fish is contained in a small volume of water which makes focusing the camera easy. However, as this small tank is not open to the atmosphere, do not keep the fish like this for more than a few minutes or it may suffer from lack of oxygen. If you need to keep fish in close confinement for longer periods, it would be better to construct a less restricting container that is open at the top and bottom. Make this from three sheets of glass stuck together with aquarium sealer.

Below: *Using an electronic flash is ideal but it can show up in the final photograph as a disturbing reflection off the front glass.*

Below: *Changing the angle of the flashgun, or camera and flashgun, can eliminate reflections and produce a much better result.*

Above: *A selection of home-made mini tanks for fish photography. These are simple to make from glass and silicone sealant.*

Goldfish varieties

Your local aquarium shop should stock a selection of the most common varieties of goldfish, but it can be difficult to select the ones best suited for your bowl or aquarium. It is easy to let the colours and strange shapes of fancy goldfish influence your choice, but it is important to consider the future welfare of the fish. If you are a beginner, err on the side of caution by choosing only the hardier varieties, such as the Common Goldfish, Fantails and small Shubunkins. Once you have gained some experience with the hardier varieties you can attempt to keep the more fancy forms. Remember that certain fancy varieties are best kept in an aquarium on their own, and some may be particularly sensitive to prolonged periods of low temperatures.

Always choose healthy, alert fish. Check that the fins are well shaped and not clamped close to the body. Make sure that the body is free from any damage, spots or abrasions and that the

eyes are clear. Avoid very lethargic fish, as well as fish with hollow bellies or sunken eyes. Beware of buying fish from tanks that contain large numbers of sick-looking or diseased fish. It is always a good sign if the fishes are feeding well.

The aquarium dealer will probably put your fishes in a plastic bag containing about one-third water and two-thirds air. Under most circumstances, this will be fine for a journey of an hour or two. However, if the journey is likely to be longer than this, ask the shop assistant to help by putting fewer fish in each bag, by using a larger bag or even by inflating the bag with oxygen rather than air. Goldfish are quite hardy but, like many fish, they are susceptible to sudden temperature fluctuations. It is important, therefore, to prevent the fish from becoming chilled or overheated during the journey home. During long journeys put the bag in a cardboard box wrapped in newspaper or in an insulated box.

Goldfish are available in over 100 different varieties. The features which distinguish them, such as coloration, body shape, finnage and the size and shape of the eyes, are the result of many years of selective breeding. Not everyone will find all the varieties attractive, but as there is such a wide choice, you should find at least one variety to suit you.

This section describes a selection of the most popular goldfish varieties.

Common Goldfish
The Common Goldfish is familiar to everyone. It has an evenly proportioned body and fins and may grow to about 23cm (9in), although it is usually much smaller if kept in a bowl or aquarium. The highest point of the shoulder should be above the pelvic fins, just before the start of the dorsal fin. The Common Goldfish has a shallow fork to its short tail fin.

A good specimen has metallic scales over the whole of the body. Yellow, red, orange, silver and even variegated fish are common.

Above: **Common Goldfish**
A classic example of this robust and handsome beginner's fish.

Below: **Common Goldfish**
*A striking variation on a theme,
with black edges to the fins.*

The Wakin is the Common
Goldfish of Japan (although it
originated in China). It is similar to
the fish described above, but has a
double tail fin. The Wakin may also
occur with nacreous scales.

The Butterfly Tail Goldfish, or
Jikin, is thought to have been
developed from the Wakin and is
rather similar to it. However, when
viewed from behind, its double tail
fin has a pronounced 'X' shape.

A relatively recent, and possibly
American, development is the
Comet-tailed Goldfish, or Comet.
This is also very similar to the
Common Goldfish, but has a long
and deeply forked tail fin. Yellow,
orange and red forms are
common. The Tancho Singletail is
similar to the Comet Tail, but it has
a silver body and fins, with a red
patch on the head.

All of these goldfish are hardy
and relatively easy to care for.
However, as a result of its active
nature, the large Comet-tailed
Goldfish is best suited to an
outdoor pool.

Photo overleaf: **Young Comet**

77

The Common Goldfish shown above provides a useful comparison for the London Shubunkin at above right and the Bristol Shubunkin shown at right, which has a significantly larger tail.

Shubunkin

Shubunkins, or Calico Goldfish, are beautiful and hardy fish. They have nacreous scales, i.e. pearly in appearance, and may reach 15cm (6in) or so in body length (23cm/9in in overall length).

The London Shubunkin has a body and fins similar to the Common Goldfish. It should have patches of red, yellow and black, along with dark speckles, on a bright blue background. This coloration and speckling usually extends over the fins of this very attractive fish.

Bristol Shubunkins are slim fish with well-developed fins. The tail fin, in particular, should be large and forked, with rounded ends. Its coloration is identical to the London Shubunkin.

Left and below left:
Bristol Shubunkins
Two examples of this popular variety celebrated for its pearly sheen and colourful markings.

Ryukin and Tosakin
The Ryukin is a short, deep-bodied fish with a hump in the shoulder region. It has metallic scales and relatively long fins. The tail fin is forked and divided, and the anal fins are paired. This variety is quite hardy and very popular in Japan.

The Tosakin may be a development from the Ryukin. It is also known as the Peacock Tail, because of its long and forward-curled tail fin. The Tosakin appears to be rather delicate and is quite difficult to breed. Because of its difficulty in swimming, the Tosakin needs to be hand spawned (see pages 54-56 for details).

The Demekin, or Telescope-eyed Goldfish is also similar to the Ryukin, but it has large protruding telescope eyes. This fish occurs in black and red, and in both metallic and nacreous forms.

Below and overleaf: **Ryukin**
This variety has a pronounced hump to the shoulder and attractive finnage. Below, a white form; overleaf, a white and red.

Left: **Red Ryukin**
*A fine example of this twintail
variety showing its characteristic
flowing fins and short, deep body.*

Top and above: *This view of a
Tosakin (top) emphasizes its
splendid tail. Below it, a
Telescope-eyed Calico Goldfish.*

Above: **Blue-scaled Telescope Eye**
*A particularly attractive specimen
of this striking variety.*

Below: **Calico Telescope Eye**
*The eyes of these forms may take
up to six months to develop fully.*

Above: **Bronze Fantail**
A one-year old specimen of this very popular goldfish variety.

Below: **Jikin**
A rear view shows why this Fantail is also known as Butterfly Tail.

Fantail
The Fantail is the western form of the Ryukin. It may have either metallic or nacreous scales, and normal or telescope eyes. This variety has an egg-shaped body and no shoulder hump. It has double anal and tail fins, with the finnage somewhat less well developed than in the Ryukin.

To breed good-quality Fantails, rigorous selection of the fry is necessary, especially if your fish are to have the characteristic high dorsal fin. Fantail goldfish can be sensitive to prolonged exposure to low temperatures. Ideally, keep them at a temperature in the range 13-21°C (55-70°F).

Overleaf: **Fantail**
A superb variety for an aquarium.

Above: **Calico Fantail**
An attractive combination of colour patterning and splendid finnage.

Below: **Red Scaled Fantail**
This is the metallic-scaled form. Nacreous varieties are also seen.

Veiltail

The Veiltail is a particularly beautiful and graceful fish that was developed in the USA during the early 1900s. It rarely grows beyond 20cm (8in) in length, including the fins. It is a round, deep-bodied fish, with a well-developed dorsal fin. It may have metallic or nacreous scales, and either normal or telescope eyes. The long trailing tail fin, which is fully divided, is

Above: **Orange Veiltail**
The trailing tail fin and prominent dorsal fin are typical features.

easily damaged. The anal fins are paired and are quite well developed, as are the other fins.

This fish is also susceptible to low temperatures, and the telescope-eyed form may have difficulty competing for food with more active fish.

Above: **Brown Veiltail**
This subtle colour is an attractive variation on the usual orange and gold theme seen in many fancy goldfishes. The Veiltail is a well-established form and a particularly popular show fish.

Top right: **Calico Veiltail**
A well-finned fish at five months.

Right: **Metallic Veiltail**
An 'uncoloured' form of this fish.

Overleaf: **Calico Veiltail**

Moor

The Moor (or Black Moor, as it is often called) is a metallic-scaled, black veiltailed variety. It may lose its velvet-like appearance with increasing age. Protect from prolonged low temperatures.

Oranda

The Oranda is a metallic-scaled fish, somewhat similar in appearance to the Veiltail. However, the head is encased in a prominent 'hood' – a raspberry-like outgrowth of skin. This should encase the whole head, with the exception of the eyes and mouth. The Oranda may grow to 20-25cm (8-10in) in length, including the fins. Protect it from low temperatures and the attentions of other very active fish. The Azumanishiki is the very attractive nacreous form of the Oranda.

The Red-cap Oranda has a silvery body with an obvious red 'cap' on the forehead. Quite hardy.

Below: **Oranda**
A splendid form, popular for its graceful and striking appearance.

Above: **Moor (3 months old)**

Right: **Brocaded Calico Oranda**

Above:
Orange and White Calico Oranda
A fine fusion of colour and form.

Right: **Red Cap (Tancho) Oranda**
*The red outgrowths on the head
show up well on the white body.*

Lionhead and Ranchu

The Lionhead is also hooded. This variety rarely grows beyond 15cm (6in), including the fins, and it may have either metallic or nacreous scales. It has a short, deep body with an arched back and no dorsal fin. The other fins are short and the anal fins are paired. The double tail fin should not droop, and its upper edges should be held away from the body. The development of the hood may vary, but is usually more pronounced in males, who may periodically shed patches of their hood.

The Ranchu is a Japanese development of the Lionhead, with a more downturned tail and tail fin. The Edonishiki is the nacreous form of the Ranchu.

Lionheads are sometimes sensitive to low temperatures.

Above and overleaf: **Ranchu**
Beautiful forms of the Lionhead.

Right:
White/Red Chinese Lionhead
A very striking colour combination.

Below: **Lionhead Goldfish**

Pompon

This variety is similar in body shape and finnage to the Lionhead but, instead of a hood, it has bundles of loose fleshy outgrowths between the nostrils, on each side of the head. The extent of these outgrowths, which are enlargements of each nasal septum, varies considerably; in some fish they hang down past the mouth. The Pompon has metallic or nacreous scales, and can occur with or without a dorsal fin.

Celestial

The Celestial has similar finnage to the Ryukin and Fantail, but it has enlarged telescope eyes which turn upwards, giving the fish its name. (The eyes are normal in newly born individuals and turn upwards as the fish matures.) It may have either metallic or nacreous scales. The Celestial is rather delicate, being quite sensitive to the cold. Since it cannot compete with more active fish for food, it is best to keep this variety on its own.

The Toadhead (also known by the Japanese name of Hama-Tou) is similar to the Celestial but has more normal-looking eyes, each with a small bladder-like growth beneath it.

Above: **Pompon Goldfish**
In a prize-winning specimen, the nasal outgrowths should be equal.

Above: **White Pompon Oranda**
This elegant form, also known as Hanafusa, has a dorsal fin.

Below: **Celestial Goldfish**
This aptly named form has telescope eyes that turn upwards.

Bubble-eye

This is usually a metallic-scaled fish somewhat similar to the Celestial. Beneath each otherwise normal-looking eye is a large fluid-filled bladder, which moves when the fish swims.

Like the Celestial, the Bubble-eye is also delicate, and sharp-edged rocks and tank decorations can easily damage the eye-bladders. However, these usually repair themselves with time.

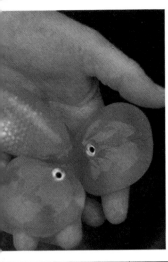

Far left: **Calico Bubble-eye**
Remarkable form and fine colour.

Left and below: *These pictures emphasize the size of the eye bladders of Bubble-eye Goldfishes.*

Left: **Orange/White Bubble-eye**
Note the absence of a dorsal fin.

Overleaf: **Orange/Gold Bubble-eye**
A fine specimen of this variety.

Above: **Calico Pearlscale**
Note the typical domed scales.

Pearlscale
The Pearlscale is a spherical-bodied fish with finnage similar to that of the Fantail. The characteristic feature of this variety is its domed scales, which have a pearl-like appearance. Pearlscales are very susceptible to the cold and therefore should not be kept below 13°C (55°F) for long periods in the aquarium.

Other varieties

Many other varieties of goldfish have been reported and continue to be developed by specialist breeders. For example, the rather strange-looking Meteor, which has no tail fin; the Egg-fish, which lacks a dorsal fin and has a pronounced egg-shaped body; and the very delicate Curled-gill, which owes its name to the out-turned appearance of its gill covers. Enthusiasts worldwide continue to celebrate the goldfish.

Index to species

Page numbers in **bold** indicate major references, including accompanying photographs. Page numbers in *italics* indicate captions to other illustrations. Less important text entries are shown in normal type.

Picture credits

Artists
Copyright of the artwork illustrations on the pages following the artist's name is the property of Salamander Books Ltd.

Brian Watson (Linden Artists) 12, 15, 16, 19, 20, 21, 26, 28, 29, 42, 43, 55, 58, 67, 71

Photographs
The publishers wish to thank the following photographers and agencies who have supplied photographs for this book. The photographs have been credited by page number and position on the page: (B)Bottom, (T)Top, (C)Centre, (BL)Bottom left etc.

David Allison: 98(B)

Dr. Chris Andrews: 14, 57, 60(B), 64(C,B), 65(C)

Heather Angel/Biofotos: 10-11, 17, 74-5, 76-7(T)

Vic Capaldi: 21, 33, 39(B), 56, 82(T,B), 92(T,B), 95(B), 102-3(B)

Eric Crichton © Salamander Books: 25, 30(T), 36-7(B), 39(T)

Bob Esson: 49(T), 73(T), 87(T)

Ideas into Print: 22-3, 25, 37(T), 68-9, 72, 73(B)

Jan-Eric Larsson: 65(T)

Robert Mertlich: 61

Tom Moore 49(B), 50-1(T,B), 89(T), 95(T), 96-7, 99(T)

Laurence Perkins 30(B)

Fred Rosenzweig: Endpapers, Half-title page, Title page, Copyright page, 15, 18, 31, 32, 41, 46, 59, 60(T), 63, 76-7(B), 78-9, 80(T), 80-1(B), 83, 84-5, 87(B), 88(T,B), 90-1, 93, 94, 99(B), 100, 101, 102(T), 103(T), 104-5, 107(T), 106-7(B), 108(T,B), 109(T,B), 110-11, 112-13

David Sands: 62

Peter W. Scott: 65(B)

Terry Waller © Salamander Books: 48, 66

Pam Whittington: 47, 49(C), 81(T), 89(B), 106(T)

Acknowledgements
The publishers wish to thank Colin Pannell and FBAS; Linda Miller, Ash Green Village Petshop; Karen Ramsay for editorial assistance.

Author's acknowledgements
The author wishes to thank Jackie King and Cliff Nash of Tetra UK, and Shelley Couper, for their help and assistance in the preparation of this book.

Further reading

Books

Brown, E.E. and Gratzek, J.B. *Fish Farming Handbook* AVI Publishing Company

Carrington, J.N. *A Fishkeeper's Guide to Maintaining a Healthy Aquarium* Salamander Books

Emmanuel, W.D. and Mannheim, L.A. *The All-in-One Camera Book* Focal Press

Hearne, T. *Caring for Your Goldfish* Collins/R.S.P.C.A.

Hervey, G.F. and Hems, J. *The Goldfish* Faber

Ladiges, W. *Coldwater Fish in the Home and Garden* Tetra Press

Mills, D. *You and Your Aquarium* Dorling and Kindersley

Moyle, P.M. and Cech, J.J. *Fishes – An Introduction to Ichthyology* Prentice Hall

Muus, B. and Dahlstrom, P. *Collins Guide to Freshwater Fishes of Britain and Europe* Collins

Orme, F. *Fancy Goldfish Culture* Saiga Publishing

Sterber, G. *The Aquarists Encyclopedia* Blandford Press

de Thabrew, V. *Coldwater Aquarium Plants* Thornhill Press

Magazines

Amateur Photographer Surrey House, 1 Throwley Way, Sutton, Surrey SM1 4QQ, England

Aquarist and Pondkeeper Buckley Press, Half Acre, Brentford TW8 8BN, England

Aquarium Digest Tetra, 201 Tabor Road, Morris Plains, N.J. 07950, U.S.A.

Freshwater and Marine Aquarium Magazine P.O. Box 487, Sierra Madre, California 91024, U.S.A.

Practical Fishkeeping EMAP National Publications, Bretton Court, Bretton, Peterborough PE3 8DZ, England

Specialist Societies

Details of local Goldfish Societies can be found in the above aquatic magazines.